DANCING ON THE WATER

Stories from the Mission Field

D.W. Hansen

Tulsa, Oklahoma | Guadalajara, Mexico
Tepic, Mexico

Dancing on the Water
© 2025 by Dwight (D.W.) Hansen

Published by Grafo House Publishing
in conjunction with Heart4Mexico
Tulsa, Oklahoma | Guadalajara, Mexico

Hardbound ISBN 978-1-963127-36-2
Paperback ISBN 978-1-963127-34-8
Ebook ISBN 978-1-963127-35-5

To contact the author or inquire about bulk discounts for churches and Bible study groups, visit h4mx.org.

Worldwide rights reserved. No part of this publication may be reproduced, stored in a retrieval system, or transmitted, in any form or by any means, without written consent from the publisher. The views and opinions expressed herein are solely those of the author and not necessarily those of the publishers.

Unless otherwise indicated, all Scripture quotations are taken from the Holy Bible, New King James Version. Copyright © 1982 by Thomas Nelson, Inc. Used by permission. All rights reserved.

Scriptures marked NASB are taken from the Holy Bible, New American Standard Bible, Copyright © 1960, 1971, 1977, 1995, 2020 by The Lockman Foundation. All rights reserved.

Printed in the United States of America
28 27 26 25   1 2 3 4

You never dance on the water alone.

*To my loving wife, Mary Jo—your steady hand
and fearless faith have been with me every step,
through calm seas and crashing waves.*

*And to our amazing children, Jesiah and Rebecca,
who serve with us in the ministry—thank you for
sharing the calling, the cost, and the joy.*

*These are our stories.
And together, we are dancing on the water.*

CONTENTS

Preface	3
1. To Russia, with Love	5
2. The First One to Dance	25
3. The Invitation	49
4. Jump In	71
5. He Upholds All Things	89
6. Move Every Obstacle	105
7. Keep Looking at Jesus	127
8. We Never Look Back, and We Don't Look Down	147
9. Wrong Thinking Leads to Sinking	165
10. I'm Dancing Now	183
About the Author	197

The murky water made it impossible to see beneath the surface, and the wind whipped the waves into a frenzy. I knew these unpredictable waters well; I grew up on this sea and had fished it all my life. But right now, it was hostile, treacherous, and dark.

Suddenly, a chill ran down my spine: a figure was walking on the water in the middle of the storm. Everyone thought it had to be a ghost, but as fear gripped us, the figure spoke: "Be of good cheer, it is I; do not be afraid." It was Jesus' voice, but was it really Him?

The guys in the boat were stunned, too shocked to speak—at least nothing I could hear over the roar of the wind. I called out, asking Him to command me to come to Him.

The only thing that pierced through the chaos was His voice.

"Come."

Without thinking much, I stepped out. I've always been impulsive, often jumping before thinking, and this was no different. With my eyes locked on Jesus, I felt the water beneath my feet become as solid as the ground. I was a fisherman but had never experienced the water like this. He was walking on the water, and when He invited me, I walked on the water too.

But soon, the roar of the wind grew louder, drowning out everything else, even His call to come to Him. "This is impossible; no one does this," I thought. Against all the warnings to keep my eyes on Him, I looked down. The moment I did, I felt my foot slip beneath the surface, and panic set in. I was sinking. My doubt paralyzed me, and I sank despite being a strong swimmer.

"Lord, save me," I cried out. Instantly, His strong hand caught hold of me. He always catches us when we fall.

Then, He asked me why I doubted, a question that struck deep within me. I had everything going for me: He made walking on water look effortless, never faltering, setting the perfect example. He had invited me to come, and He has the authority to do that. The wind even ceased as soon as we got back into the boat.

I had taken those first few steps, so why did I doubt? Later, I realized that He always desires our faith and trust in His word. If He says, "Come," then there is no reason to doubt. His invitation always carries the power to fulfill it.

—Simon Bar-Jonah, a.k.a. Peter

PREFACE

"It is an insult not to trust the Lord after so many years of miracles. After all He has done, the one thing the Lord deserves from us is faith and trust. *Once you have walked on the water long enough, you can dance on the water.*"

These words formed the heart of a sermon I preached at our church one Sunday in 2015. The phrase "dancing on the water" quickly became part of our church's vocabulary. My daughter-in-law, Mimi, was even inspired to compose a song with that as its title.

Over the years, the Lord has sustained us as we walked in faith. As the old hymn says, we have already come through many dangers, trials, and snares. How can we doubt after all we have been through? The Lord has been faithful, protecting and providing every step of the way. These experiences have taught us that after all we've been through, the Lord truly deserves our unwavering faith and trust.

One way to ensure we will keep trusting or "keep the faith" is by remembering His power and faithfulness.

> "Once you have walked on the water long enough, you can dance on the water."

> *Remember His marvelous works which He has done,*
> *His wonders, and the judgments of His mouth.*
> *(Psalm 105:5)*

We must tell the stories repeatedly. My goal in this book is to remember and record what the Lord has done in our lives as we walk by faith.

I have heard many incredible and unique stories from missionaries and fellow Christians. I could fill this book with their stories and we would all stand amazed at what the Lord has done in and through so many great servants of Jesus. The most incredible adventures and true stories are the ones we share about what the Lord has done through us. "But the people who know their God shall be strong, and carry out great exploits" (Daniel 11:32).

Like Peter, the Lord calls us to walk by faith. As William Carey said, "Attempt great things for God; expect great things from God." When Christ calls us, we need to step out of the boat and walk on the water by faith.

Here's the fun part: once you walk on water often enough, you get used to it. You fall in love with it. You start to look for it, expect it, and enjoy it. And then, you start dancing on it as you rejoice in God's ongoing, unfailing faithfulness.

Walking on water is a great start, but *dancing* on water is meant to be the story of your life.

CHAPTER 1
TO RUSSIA WITH LOVE

And He said to them, "Go into all the world and preach the gospel to every creature."

Mark 16:15

The travel agent's eyes nearly popped with surprise as we set wads of crisp bills on his desk, counting them meticulously. "The ticket total is $11,000," he stated, his voice tinged with curiosity.

We kept counting, the tension mounting with each bill we laid down: "$8,000, $9,000, $10,000." The atmosphere was electric—we were so close, just a breath away from our goal. Then, as if on cue, the phone rang. It was a lifeline, a pledge for $500. The agent, sensing our determination and perhaps moved by our cause, leaned in and offered to cover the shortfall until the pledged money arrived. With tickets finally in hand, we bolted out of there, racing against the clock to make our flight—first stop, Tokyo, and then onward to the Soviet Union.

Our mad dash for the airplane was the culmination of months of work and faith. It was the summer of 1980, marked by the Olympic Games in Moscow. However, President Carter's boycott postponed our trip until the games concluded. Our mission, which we called "Operation Friendship," was orchestrated by Youth With A Mission (YWAM). It was a bold endeavor to spread the good news in lands that often regarded outsiders with suspicion. The USSR was particularly resistant to the gospel, but the Olympic Games had unexpectedly flung open the gates—160 cities were now accessible to tourists for the first time in years. It was an unprecedented opportunity.

We had meticulously planned our trip for July, fresh off an outreach trip to Canada. With visas for the USSR in hand and passports secured, everything seemed to fall into place. But one daunting hurdle remained—we did not have the money to pay for the trip. Faced with this challenge, our team prayed, seeking divine guidance. The Lord gave us a passage from Habakkuk:

> *Though the fig tree may not blossom,*
> *Nor fruit be on the vines;*
> *Though the labor of the olive may fail,*
> *And the fields yield no food;*
> *Though the flock may be cut off from the fold,*
> *And there be no herd in the stalls—*
> *Yet I will rejoice in the LORD,*
> *I will joy in the God of my salvation."*
> *(Habakkuk 3:17–18)*

With renewed faith, we made the difficult decision to reschedule our trip for August. We met every Monday night to pray and share updates on our fundraising efforts. Each gathering strengthened our resolve and moved us closer to fulfilling our mission.

Our team consisted of five individuals—three young women (one of whom was a single mother), me, and our leader, Steve. We spent months in fervent prayer and relentless fundraising. After much effort, I secured my $2,200 share and felt confident and ready for the journey ahead. However, the single mother in our group hadn't raised a single penny. I remember thinking, *It's not right for her to leave her child for over a month.*

> "Give half your funds to the single mother."

Yet, we had made a pact as a team: If one of us couldn't go, none would. During an intense moment of prayer, I felt the Lord say, "Give half your funds to the single mother."

At first, I hesitated to give up half my money, wondering if I'd regret it. But once I finally did, it felt great. And then, something incredible happened—it was like the floodgates of heaven opened! Just three days before our flight, $5,500 came in. The generosity we experienced was beyond anything I could have imagined—a powerful reminder that amazing things follow when you take a step of faith.

We had to prepay for our trip, which covered airfare and other travel costs—but not food. We spent every penny, leaving one big question: How would we eat? None of us had a credit card or other means to pay for food. Still, the excitement of my first international flight drowned out any worries. It all felt more like a dream than real life.

First Stop: Tokyo

The eleven-hour flight to Tokyo passed quickly. We prayed as a team, shared the gospel with our fellow passengers, and immersed ourselves in Scripture. At one point, I found myself reading Psalm 105:19:

> *Until the time that his word came to pass,*
> *The word of the* L<small>ORD</small> *tested him.*

A thought struck me: *God will test His word to us on this trip.* It was a reminder that this journey was not just about reaching a destination but about testing the faith and promises we held on to.

Since we had no money, we decided to sleep at the airport. Exhausted, we found a corner with benches, and I fell asleep. I always could sleep in difficult places, but this was the worst.

Soon, I was startled awake to find us surrounded by stern-looking police. They commanded us to go with them, and we hesitantly obeyed. They moved us to a quieter location, and when we were settled, they laughed at how scared we looked when they woke us. We joined in the laughter but did not sleep much after that.

There was a significant snag in our plans, a detail I haven't mentioned yet. Because we rescheduled the trip for August, our visas for the USSR needed to be reissued, but they did not arrive on time for our flight. "I'll send them on tomorrow's plane," our travel agent assured us before we left Seattle. "You'll get them in time to catch your next flight out of Tokyo."

As the clock ticked down in the Tokyo airport, we waited anxiously, clinging to hope and prayer, trusting that the day's flight from Seattle would deliver the visas. But as the hours passed, our anxiety grew, matched only by our growing hunger—we had no food and no certainty.

When the afternoon flight finally touched down, we received the bad news that our visas were not on board. Our hopes were dashed, and we wondered what would happen if we flew into Russia without the essential documents.

Our travel schedule meant we had to move to another airport on the other side of Tokyo, where we spent the night waiting for our next flight. Once again, sleep was difficult, as more stern-faced guards woke us and made us move on. We believed this was another test from God—to see if we could endure without complaining.

Next Stop: Niigata

The following day, we flew across Japan, destined for a small airport called Niigata, on the country's west coast. After a few hours' layover, we would board a flight bound for Khabarovsk, Siberia, deep in the USSR.

Doubts and warnings from others echoed in our ears: "Without visas, they will never let you into the USSR."

But Steve, our leader, was unshakable. "God told us to go, so we will go until we can't go further," he declared.

As the hours dragged on, hunger gnawed at us. My mouth watered when the flight attendant handed out warm towels. *Surely, this is to prepare us for a meal*, I thought. But no food came, and we landed with empty stomachs.

With just a few hours left before our flight to Siberia, we approached the counter of the Soviet airline Aeroflot and handed the agent our tickets.

"Visas, please," he requested.

"Yeah, about that…Um, we have visas—they were issued—but we don't have them on us," we explained.

The agent's response was firm: "You cannot go to the USSR without a visa. If I let you board the plane, you'll be detained upon arrival, placed in jail, and sent back to us on the next flight, which is in one week."

We tried to plead our case, but it was useless. Defeated, we slumped down in the waiting area. The girls went to the bathroom to cry, and, honestly, I did too. When I returned, I noticed a strange, determined look in Steve's eyes.

"God told us to go to Russia, right?" he said, his voice filled with conviction. "He never said what we would do there. I say we go, even if we stay in jail for a week."

The daring of youth often treads the line between courage and recklessness. Fueled by faith and adrenaline (and a good dose of ignorance), we were seriously considering such a risky plan. To the girls, the idea was even more terrifying.

> "You guys are nuts!"

Unable to hide her fear, one of them blurted out, "You guys are nuts!"

With his piercing gaze, Steve asked, "Is that your fear speaking, or the Lord?"

"It's all me," she confessed, "I'm petrified."

We approached the counter with renewed determination, hoping to convince the agent to allow us to board. The official stood firm. "You will be imprisoned if you continue without visas," he warned.

"Then let us go and face the consequences," we responded.

The agent's perplexed expression suggested he thought we were out of our minds. The conversation spiraled in circles, neither side willing to concede.

Finally, in a moment of clarity amid the back-and-forth, I asked, "Is our flight still here?"

His brief response, "No, it's gone," hit like a gut punch.

Now, what were we going to do? We were stranded on the west coast of Japan, penniless and ravenous.

A torrent of thoughts rushed through my mind. *How on earth am I supposed to get home from here? Hitch-hiking from Japan isn't an option.* The enormity of our situation began to sink in.

The girls retreated to the restroom again, their eyes filled with tears, while I went for a walk in a wooded area near the airport. As I wandered down a trail, an enormous spiderweb blocked my path, with a giant spider at its center. Shivers went down my spine. I considered alternate routes, but similar spiderwebs stood to my right and left. My only recourse was to retrace my steps.

The trail felt like a metaphor for our disastrous journey: each step forward met with a barrier. Unlike the forest, though, retracing our steps was impossible. In my pre-Christian days, I trusted in drugs, relationships, and even criminal acts, but it all proved futile. I muttered to myself, *Nothing I put my trust in works out, and now even Jesus has failed me.* I thought about this and much more on that path of spiderwebs. With a sinking heart and an empty stomach, I headed back, the weight of hopelessness heavy on my shoulders.

Regrouping at the small airport, we collectively decided to hunker down, hoping for a door to open. We settled onto the benches, preparing for another night sleeping in an airport. As we got comfortable, a kind Japan Airlines agent named Akihiko approached us. He spoke fluent English and, with a gentle but firm tone, informed us, "You cannot spend the night here. This airport closes at 9:30 p.m."

We explained our situation, emphasizing that we had exhausted our prepaid travel funds. His concern for us was evident, but he said, "You'll need to stay outside."

As the words left his mouth, the skies opened, and it began to pour. Akihiko glanced outside at the downpour, and his expression softened. "All right," he relented, "I can offer you shelter for the night. Moreover, I'll cover your train fare back to Tokyo tomorrow."

"We promise to reimburse you," we assured him, then we followed our new friend to his vehicle, which took us to a warehouse. As a cherry on top, he provided a meal. Hunger pangs were forgotten; after forty-eight hours without much food, it tasted like the most sumptuous feast I had ever had.

Back to Tokyo

I still vividly remember that grueling all-night train ride back to Tokyo. We traveled from 11:30 p.m. to 5:00 a.m. The economy train was equipped with hard benches with straight, unforgiving backs, making it impossible to find any comfortable sleeping position. I was delirious from lack of sleep and the meager food we had managed over the past four days. At one point, desperation overcame any sense of shame, and I laid down on the floor in the aisle, surrounded by cigarette butts, discarded gum, and who knows what else.

Once we finally arrived in Tokyo, the challenge continued. We had to navigate the complex web of commuter trains to reach a neighborhood on the far side of town. Each route was identified by color. "Take the Blue line to the Brown line, then catch the Green line," they instructed us. We felt like rats in a maze, sprinting on and off trains, barely catching each connection in time. Despite every obstacle, we finally made it to our contact's small home, worn out but relieved to have arrived.

In Tokyo, we found relief. Our local contact let us stay in a quaint place that soon became a spiritual sanctuary. The heavens felt close in that place, and a new plan slowly came together.

Shortly after we settled in, Steve met with a veteran missionary who traveled extensively in the USSR, China, and Mongolia and had some insight into our unexpected delay. "I tried to reach you when I heard of your journey," the man explained, "but you had already left Tokyo. I believe your mission for this trip needs to focus on Mongolia. It's one of the most closed nations to the gospel. The Christian community there is almost nonexistent, with only one known believer."

> "Preaching the gospel is illegal there. The possession of a Bible could get you arrested."

"I believe your calling is to pray at the war memorial in the capital city of Ulaanbaatar, Mongolia."

Mongolia, located between China and Russia, was entrenched in deep-rooted Buddhism and Shamanism. However, ever since the 1921 communist revolution, it had witnessed a forced shift toward atheism. The area was known as the eastern steppes, and it still harbored a nomadic way of life where the human population was outnumbered by goats and horses.

The veteran missionary warned Steve, "Preaching the gospel is illegal there. The possession of a Bible could get you arrested."

Our journey plan completely changed after we visited the Russian embassy. We revamped our itinerary, prioritizing our time in Mongolia. Given the risks of carrying our Bibles, we opted for caution and left them behind in Tokyo. Comforted by the verses I had committed to memory, I entrusted my Bible to our gracious Tokyo contact.

In what seemed like divine intervention, funds from home arrived just in time that week, which meant we could pay for our updated itinerary. Our travel agent expedited our renewed visas, and upon our return to the Tokyo airport, they were handed to us, making the continued journey possible.

The following week, we returned to Niigata Airport, this time with confidence. The reaction from the airport staff was almost comical—*They're back!* The look of surprise on our friend's face was just as priceless when we gratefully paid him back for the train tickets.

"Visas, please," the same ticket agent as the week before asked. We triumphantly handed them over, enjoying his astonishment. And soon we boarded the plane on our journey to Khabarovsk, USSR.

Into Siberia

Siberia's reputation preceded it—a land synonymous with biting cold and icy expanses. The chilly air and frost emanating from the vents inside the plane confirmed these tales. As the tune "The Entertainer" from the 1973 film *The Sting* played, our plane bounced and skipped down the runway until it came to a stop. But stepping out, the reality was starkly different—a balmy

80 degrees welcomed us, debunking every myth I held about Siberia.

Riding the Trans-Siberian Railroad for three days without food or the ability to converse in Russian was nothing short of an ordeal. The train's layout was simple: two bunk beds per room. Unlike in the U.S., there was no privacy on the train. The women in our group had three beds, and a male traveler took the fourth. Steve bunked in the same room as a couple, and I was with an old lady. Our roommates changed as people boarded or disembarked. Always looking for an opportunity to share the gospel, I viewed these chance encounters as divine appointments.

I still remember well one particular guy—a lieutenant from the Red Army. Determined to bridge the language barrier, I employed every communication strategy I knew. With my guitar in tow (I still can't believe I carried it on that trip), I tried to break the ice by playing him a Russian song I had learned. But he remained unmoved, his expression stoic.

Out of the blue, he broke his silence. "Do you want to see my pictures?" he asked in clear, fluent English.

I was taken aback. As I tried to communicate, he understood me perfectly. Eager to learn more about him, I enthusiastically agreed. He retrieved a box stashed beneath his bunk and showed me photographs of his loved ones.

Looking back on that encounter with the lieutenant, I started understanding our cultural gap. He wore the standard-issue Red Army uniform—a look we'd seen repeatedly during our travels. Meanwhile, we Westerners stood out in our fresh sneakers, blue jeans, and all the little things that screamed individuality. I could imagine how that might have felt overwhelming to him.

> He was a real person with hopes, struggles, and needs like mine.

As I tried to share bits of my unique background, I could have unintentionally made him feel more out of place—or maybe even overshadowed. In his world, where standing out is rare and sometimes outright discouraged, he probably struggled to find something that felt genuinely his.

And then it hit him: his photographs. Those snapshots were his treasures, untouched by government propaganda or the push to conform. They were his story, tucked away in a system that celebrated the collective over the individual.

My encounter with the lieutenant opened my eyes to how deeply everyone needs Jesus. He wasn't just a uniformed officer or a faceless part of the system—he was a real person with hopes, struggles, and needs like mine.

Finally, Mongolia

Food! Excellent sweet food! The hotel in Mongolia included meals. Well, they first told us we would have to return to the USSR hungry because our food vouchers were never sent. Soon, though, they found the vouchers, and our tour guide laughed at us because they sent way more than we needed.

Our trip through Siberia did not include meals, so we survived on a few things we brought along and the complimentary tea the train provided. I was skinny when I left for the trip, and I had lost fifteen pounds by the time it was over. I had to pace myself when the tender meat and a cup of yogurt arrived. Later, I discovered the meat was sheep's tongue, and the drink was *tarag*, a popular Mongolian beverage.

In Mongolia, our primary objective was to pray for divine encounters while being ready if opportunities arose to spread the gospel. We were cautious, aware of the need to avoid arrest and the potential for being caught in the crossfire of the political conflict between communism and capitalism. We understood that our battle was not against individuals or the government but against unseen spiritual forces. Opening Mongolia to the good news was crucial, so our prayers were focused on creating pathways for the gospel.

Throughout our time in Mongolia, I couldn't shake off an eerie sense of surveillance. Our cheerful tour guide, Koa-Koa, who spoke fluent English, was perpetually by our side. Despite her friendly demeanor, it became clear that her role wasn't merely to guide us but also to monitor our activities.

One evening, we wandered a local park without her watchful gaze. The sense of freedom was refreshing, and we began leaving some literature in the seating areas. However, while we prayed and hid the Bible tracts we carried, a team member's hushed observation sent me a chill: "Someone is lurking in the shadows."

> "Someone is lurking in the shadows."

Squinting, I discerned a figure which seemed to be observing us. Then, I noticed more shadowy figures beyond the first one. Panic settled in, and images of incarceration in a bleak communist facility filled my mind.

With an attempt to look casual, we continued our walk, praying under our breath. Suddenly, as we rounded a clump of shrubs, we came face-to-face with one of the shadowy watchers. Before panic could set in again, Steve calmly remarked, "It's a statue."

A closer inspection confirmed his observation: the park was dotted with life-sized human statues. We'd let our imaginations run wild. Despite the laughable misunderstanding, a feeling of being under scrutiny lingered.

Every day, our tour guide ushered us through what felt like a propaganda-laced journey that showcased various landmarks and museums. Yet, our primary intent in Ulaanbaatar was to pray at the renowned war memorial at Zaisan Memorial Hill. To our relief, she announced a visit to this location one day. While this was a welcomed plan, I wondered how we would discreetly shout that Jesus is Lord with her by our side.

As we approached the hill, our guide pointed upward and remarked, "There are 612 steps leading to the top." I don't know if she didn't want to climb the steps or was giving us privacy, but she added, "If you don't mind, I'll wait for you here."

It was an unexpected window of opportunity, so we told her, "Of course, you can wait here," and hurriedly ascended the hill. Well, as hurriedly as we could stagger up 612 steps at 1,300 meters (4,300 feet) of altitude, anyway.

Once at the summit, we dispersed to different corners and, with conviction in our hearts, shouted, "Jesus Christ is Lord of all Mongolia." At that moment, I sensed a spiritual shift in the atmosphere. But then, glancing around, I was surprised to see our tour guide had joined us, having decided to make the climb after all. Whether she observed our act of faith or chose to overlook it, she voiced no objections. Our mission was successfully achieved.

Other groups, like ours, ventured to Mongolia, fueled by the same purpose: to pray and witness transformation. Notably, after the 1990 revolution, Mongolia embraced the gospel by modifying its constitution to grant religious freedom. Fast forward to 2023, and the country boasts a Christian community of over 40,000 and more than 600 churches. This remarkable change underscores the power of faith, demonstrating how God can work wonders through five young believers committed to their mission and countless other faithful followers of Jesus.

Though our primary mission was achieved, our journey was far from over. First, we flew back to Irkutsk in the USSR, and then we settled in for a three-day train ride to the port city of Vladivostok. Again, the ride consisted of railroad tea, no food, and many unique encounters with people who needed to know Jesus.

Cruise to Japan

Returning to Japan was an unforgettable experience. We traveled on a Russian ship, and to our delight, all-you-can-eat food was included. On the first day, the dining hall was packed with hungry diners eager to feast. But when a typhoon hit the Pacific, our small cruise ship was tossed around like a toy in the waves. The next day, the dining hall was nearly empty, with only a few green-faced passengers in sight.

I was fortunate not to get seasick and determined to make up for my involuntary fast by eating everything I could. However, my body couldn't handle the sudden feast after so many days with little food. It wasn't long before I joined the ranks of the sick people, regretting my overindulgence.

The typhoon caused a fourteen-hour delay, which meant we had to head directly to the airport from our port in Yokohama. As our friend who picked us up handed us our long-missed Bibles, he informed us, "There are tight restrictions on anyone going to the airport. All week, there have been threats from leftist guerillas, and the airport is locked down. Pray we can get through." It was amazing how many obstacles got in our way.

> If God calls you to go somewhere, buy a ticket and fly; if you can't buy the ticket, drive; if you can't drive, walk; if you can't walk, aim in the direction He calls you and fall.

I remember my mother seeing me arrive home as skinny as a rail. The joy of seeing home and family was matched by the fulfillment of knowing we had accomplished something of eternal significance.

Our trip to the Soviet Union was my first opportunity to walk on water. We walk until we can go no further. This walk took us halfway around the world and back. I heard this concept clearly expressed by someone once. "If God calls you to go somewhere, buy a ticket and fly; if you can't buy the ticket, drive; if you can't drive, walk; if you can't walk, aim in the direction He calls you and fall." That is the way five inexperienced youths traveled over 30,000 kilometers (19,000 miles). Someone more powerful than us sustained us and carried us all the way.

CHAPTER 2

THE FIRST ONE TO DANCE

Now the Lord *had said to Abram:*
"Get out of your country,
From your family
And from your father's house,
To a land that I will show you."

Genesis 12:1

Traveling to the USSR and Mongolia was my first big leap of faith. It felt like dancing on water—exciting, uncertain, and completely out of my comfort zone. As the Bible says, "The just shall live by faith" (Romans 1:17), and this trip reflected my first shaky steps in my walk with Christ.

Abraham

Abraham, the father of faith, was the trailblazer in stepping out in faith. He set the standard for walking by faith. Imagine his circumstances: he lived in Ur of the Chaldeans, believed by many to be located in modern-day southeastern Iraq, and came from a family utterly unfamiliar with the one true God. Abraham's father moved from Ur to Haran, where God called Abraham to leave his country and family and travel to a land God would show him.

He must have had his doubts, yet when God's call came to depart for an unknown destination, he heeded it. He ventured out without knowing his ultimate destination. That is walking on the water. It is walking by faith and not by sight.

Abraham stands as an example in all our missionary training because when God said "Go," he obeyed with unwavering faith. This mirrors how Jesus called His disciples. They took their first steps with a simple yet profound call—"Follow me."

Jesus extended an invitation, but He didn't tell them where he was going or what they would do. "The Son of man has nowhere to lay His head." "Let the dead bury the dead." "Take up your cross and follow me." These were some of His responses when people inquired about their destination, lodging, and provisions.

For Jesus' followers today, our steps of faith might look ridiculous to many and even foolish to others. They might ask us where we are going. They might ridicule our lack of planning and preparation. But their negativity doesn't get to determine our faith, and it certainly doesn't control God's response. As the saying goes, "Man proposes, but God disposes." We step out on the water and leave the antigravity support up to Him.

An Impossible Invitation

I was out of money following my expedition to the USSR and Mongolia. The idea of going on another journey seemed utterly impossible. So, you can imagine my surprise when I received an invitation to join a team traveling to the Mariana Islands in the Western Pacific. I told the team director that I was out of money, adding that I did not have time to gather the necessary funds. I truly believed there was no way I could go. But after praying and talking it through, the team decided to just go for it—trusting that God would take care of things along the way.

Our flight departed from Canada, so we stopped at my family home on our way to Vancouver, B.C. That evening, I talked with my father, who asked me how I would go on the trip since I had no money. I told him the truth: I had no idea but trusted God. As we left early the next day, he said, joking, "I'll see you in the afternoon."

At that point, I was doubting the trip myself. The idea of a van ride home after everyone else boarded the plane was depressing.

> I told him the truth: I had no idea but trusted God.

With less than four hours remaining before our flight's departure, we stopped at a rest area. I noticed the rest of the team engaged in conversation, and I feared they were discussing the possibility of leaving me behind at the airport. When the director called me over, I braced myself for what I thought was an inevitable outcome. However, his words took me completely by surprise.

"As a team, we discussed and made a decision concerning your participation in this trip," he began. "We decided to give our ground fees to buy your ticket."

He explained that each team member had set aside cash for food expenses, which they would sacrifice for my journey. He concluded, "We don't know how we will manage without food, but we are placing our trust in Jesus, and we believe He will provide."

I was both amazed and somewhat anxious about the situation. Having returned from my previous trip, I was already thin, and going six weeks without food seemed almost unimaginable. However, I couldn't ignore the call I felt from Jesus to follow Him, and I firmly believed He wanted me to be a part of this team.

> I was already thin, and going six weeks without food seemed almost unimaginable.

With this conviction, I put one foot in front of the other and flew off to the islands via Honolulu, Hawaii. It was my second adventure of faith in less than two years of following Jesus.

Hawaii and Beyond

Upon arriving in Hawaii, the same assurance I received in Tokyo returned, and I felt the Lord tell me: "I will carry you; I will cover you." Our team spent some time exploring and sharing with people in Hawaii.

Meanwhile, my father wondered what had happened to me since I had never returned from Canada. Of course, there were no cell phones in 1981, and international calls were costly, so it took me several days to finally make the international call home.

His immediate reaction was one of concern and confusion. "Where are you? Why didn't you come straight back home?" He expressed his worry and disbelief at my ability to go on the trip. It took some time to explain that I was in Hawaii on my way to the islands.

After our brief stay in Hawaii, we took the island hopper flight to Saipan. The flight crossed the international date line and stopped at six islands, including the Marshall Islands and Micronesia. The next day, we arrived on the stunningly beautiful island of Saipan.

Saipan is a tropical paradise with an incredible history. It was a significant Japanese base during World War II, and remnants of that era are scattered everywhere. You can find blown-up tanks in the water, abandoned bunkers hidden in the jungle, and spent shells embedded along the trails. The contrast of such a beautiful landscape with these war relics made our time there all the more impactful.

We worked daily to improve the Youth With A Mission base property and spent every afternoon and evening sharing the Gospel. Although we expected to starve, food was abundant. Long tables filled with fresh fruits, vegetables, fish, pork, beef, and chicken were our daily bread. I even helped butcher a 200-pound pig raised on coconuts, which made the meat clean and tasty.

A Trip to Tinian

"You should go to Tinian, the island just south of us. The population is small, but they need Jesus," the base leader suggested. So, we decided to take the hour-long ferry ride to the island.

Our team consisted of two couples, three single girls, and me. The couples occupied the two rooms in our cramped place while the girls made do with the living room. As for me, the only real estate left was the floor of the screened-in patio.

As I settled in for the night, I couldn't help but notice a sizable praying mantis perched on the ceiling. Its beady-eyed stare caught me off guard. Then, turning my gaze, I spotted its colossal mother, stretching over a foot long. And the surprises didn't end there. Something else caught my eye: a giant hermit crab inching toward me in the dim light accompanied by its entourage. The place was crawling with other critters—mosquitoes, rats, and cockroaches, all acting like they owned the place.

I can't handle this. There's no way I'll survive, I thought, overwhelmed by the chaotic zoo. The first day in a new place always demands adjustment, but this felt like a whole new level. Determined to find relief away from the wildlife circus, I made a beeline for the kitchen, claiming a spot on the floor to rest my weary bones. I'm sure rats and cockroaches were still nearby, but at least they weren't actively menacing me.

Tinian is a breathtaking historical place, especially because of its significant role in World War II. It's the island where the two atomic bombs were loaded before being dropped on Japan, and the remnants of overgrown airfields are still visible everywhere. The ocean particularly captivated me, and I seized every opportunity to run down to the water and snorkel in the shallow areas inside the reef.

One day, while I snorkeled, I was suddenly startled when a four-foot grey shark swam into the water inside the reef. It scared me to the bone but never bothered me.

Our time on Tinian was wonderful and enriching. Everyone we met was incredibly kind and open to the message we brought. We feasted every night, quickly becoming part of the island's vibrant community. The warmth and hospitality were unforgettable. When we returned to the United States, I was a flip-flop-wearing, sun-bronzed, tropic-loving fan of Saipan and Tinian.

You'll Find Your Bread on the Water

I also learned a lot about faith and risk, and those lessons have lasted just as long as my fond memories. Going to the airport without money was a risk, but it ultimately paid off. Over the years, I've discovered that we naturally want to control situations and manage the dangers we face. We long to witness miracles, yet we often hesitate to take the necessary risks. We tend to be overly risk-averse.

However, it's important to remember that Abraham's risk-filled journey of faith paved the way for all of us. Following Jesus is inherently risky, but as you live a life reminiscent of Abraham's, trust grows, and you realize there is no real risk when the Lord sustains you. That's what dancing on the water is all about: trusting that if God called you, He will carry you, and if He is carrying you, you can enjoy the journey...bugs and all.

> There is no real risk when the Lord sustains you. That's what dancing on the water is all about.

When coupled with trust in God's provision, faith transforms what seems like risk into a path of divine assurance. The experiences that push us out of our comfort zones are often the very ones that deepen our reliance on Him and reveal His power in our lives.

A large bank account and abundant funding are never guaranteed when walking in faith. It's as if you take a step, making yourself a candidate for provision. Just as Deuteronomy 28:2 reminds us, "All these blessings shall come upon you and overtake you, because you obey the voice of the Lord your God." The provision catches up with you along the journey.

Solomon teaches us the same concept:

> *Cast your bread upon the waters,*
> *And you will find it after many days.*
> *(Ecclesiastes 11:1)*

This may refer to ancient Egypt, where people would release their bread into the water and let it be carried downstream, where they would find it again during their journey.

As a lifelong missionary, I've had to embrace this truth constantly. My initial missionary support commitment was a mere $100 per month. When Mary Jo and I married, we could rely on just $400 per month, and we soon lost even that. Our wedding, including the dress, rings, venue, flowers, and food, cost us precisely $400. As we prepared for the event, provisions seemed to come to us from unexpected sources. It's fair to say we found our "bread on the water" on that particular day in 1984 when we were joined in marriage.

Taking that leap of faith, stepping out onto the waters, opens us up to miracles. So many of us dream of performing grand acts for God, like walking on water, yet we often overlook the everyday miracles and provisions right before us. We won't experience the extraordinary until, like Peter, we ask Jesus, "Lord, if it's You, tell me to come to You on the water."

In that moment of faith and obedience, we become receptive to the miraculous as we dare to step out despite our fears. In these acts of trust, in the willingness to step beyond the boat's safety, we encounter God's life-changing power.

A Tiny Trailer and a Desperate Prayer

Upon returning home from the islands and still having no money, the ministry road seemed to end. So, I moved back to my parents' house. Unfortunately, by then, they were using my old bedroom, so I had to stay in a little travel trailer on the side of the house.

Soon, a thick cloud of discouragement hung over me as I trudged through the daily routine, unsure of where to go next or how to regain my footing in the ministry I was called to. Maybe I needed to step up my game and improve myself, or perhaps I didn't have what it takes to serve as a minister of the gospel. Doubts swirled around me, questioning whether I was truly deserving of my wages as a worker in God's vineyard.

> One night, a troubling thought crept into my mind: Maybe God fired you.

Condemnation and self-doubt have constantly been stumbling blocks for me, and they weighed heavily on me during this time. One night, a troubling thought crept into my mind: *Maybe God fired you.* It was a dark, confusing season.

One night, after a long day at work, I came home tired and all alone. I sat in that small, run-down trailer and complained to God. "Everyone else has such a high and important calling," I lamented. "No one is even asking me to go back and serve."

In that moment of frustration and longing, I bowed down and asked God to let me serve Him. I thought of all the people I knew who God had used to change the world, and I pleaded with Him to let me do whatever He wanted me to do. I begged God for my calling.

Unlike the rich young ruler, I didn't ask what I had to give up to follow Jesus. I was willing to offer

Him everything—my life, my ambitions, my all—if He would call me. It was a moment of complete surrender, driven by a deep desire to be used for His purposes, no matter the cost.

Many people feel like they are doing God a favor by following Him. They believe they are doing Jesus a favor every time they minister. Not me! I begged for my calling and am eternally grateful for the opportunity to follow Him. My reward is not the provision or the miracle but being with Him. Like Peter, I don't want to wait in the boat; I want to dance on the water.

Thankfully, my time in the little trailer was short. I raised enough money to attend an advanced school called the School of Evangelism. There, we studied missions and unreached people groups and met wonderful missionaries. I was convinced I should go to Asia, so I continued asking the Lord for an open door.

The Exotic Land of...Hollywood?

After the school's classroom phase, we planned another exciting trip. I was beginning to develop a bit of travel lust, and the Philippines seemed like the perfect destination. At the time, we were studying unreached people groups, most of which were within a two-thousand-mile radius of Hong Kong. Asia was the place to be for missionaries, and I was eager to preach the gospel in some exotic corner of that vast continent.

I went through all the preparations, including getting the required shots and securing my visa, but the money I needed didn't come in. Out of our twenty-member team, five of us could not raise the necessary funds to go.

I was deeply disappointed when my team leader suggested we drive to Hollywood instead and serve in a street ministry called Centrum. It was the exact opposite of the exotic mission field I had envisioned. Working with runaways in Hollywood who dreamed of being discovered was far from the adventure I had hoped for. However, it was the only opportunity I could afford to pursue.

So, all five of us without funds for the Philippines piled into the ministry's 1967 Dodge van and headed to Hollywood. What I thought of as my second choice turned out to be a different kind of mission field that challenged my expectations and reshaped my understanding of what it means to serve.

Centrum was a crisis intervention ministry. We operated four homes where people could stay for a night or two while we helped them find a more stable, long-term solution. We also ran a twenty-four-hour hotline. Desperate people would call at all hours, and we would drive out to pick them up and bring them safely into one of our homes.

When I arrived, they asked me to help staff the men's home, just around the corner from Mann's

Chinese Theatre. Up to forty men stayed in this five-bedroom house, with every room packed full of people sleeping on the floor. It was wild and completely chaotic. I wouldn't say I enjoyed it, but the experience taught me a lot.

Luca, a large Italian man struggling with heroin addiction, arrived at our home one day. I vividly remember his sincere sobs as I led him to the Lord. We immediately saw an incredible change in him—he seemed like a new man, and we were all amazed at his transformation.

One day, when we planned to go to the park, Luca offered to stay back and watch the house. "You guys go ahead; I'll stay back and keep an eye on things," he said. We trusted him completely and left without a second thought.

But that sinking feeling hit me hard when we returned—Luca was gone. Not only had he left, but he had also taken a lot of stuff from the house. His conversion had been nothing more than an act, something he had perfected over time to manipulate and deceive. We soon heard from other ministries that he had done the same thing to them.

Kentay, another heroin addict, arrived at the house, and he immediately embraced the opportunity to follow Jesus. His transformation was undeniable—everyone could see the change in him. He prayed constantly, read his Bible diligently, and was always willing to help others.

One of the most touching things about Kentay was his connection with another resident who was in a wheelchair. Kentay became his devoted helper, always by his side. I still vividly remember seeing Kentay wheeling his friend around and praying for him. He was a beautiful testament to the genuine change that had taken place in his heart.

Again, we went to the park, and Kentay came along. Everyone decided to play basketball, but Kentay and I stayed on the sidelines since we were not sports guys.

"We need two more to fill the teams," one guy told us. "Come on, join in!"

So we joined and ran back and forth for a while without even touching the ball. When we took a break, while I was huffing to get air, I looked over at Kentay. He had a strange look, and then he fell to the ground, convulsing. My first thought was that he had epilepsy or something, and I began to pray, but then I noticed that he had soiled himself. Looking up, I saw a small firehouse across the park, so we ran to get help. An ambulance was there within two minutes. He was unconscious, so an EMT took him to the hospital while we returned to the house, worried and concerned.

After a while, I called the hospital for an update. "How is Kentay?" I asked the doctor after explaining my identity.

"I regret to inform you that Kentay suffered an undetermined cause of death," he said.

I could not believe it. "What? That's impossible. He was fine and doing well before this happened. What did he die from?" I asked.

The doctor informed me that there was no explanation. "It was not a heart attack or a stroke; his body just shut down, like turning off a switch. It is unexplained."

When I hung up, I saw all the men's faces. The sobering thought hit us all: "You can go anytime."

Kentay's death had a profound impact on us, and every person in the house had a come-to-Jesus moment. The next few weeks were the best times I had in the house. However, my six-week time in Hollywood was ending. I was excited to go to Hawaii, where my team leader, Steve, from the Soviet Union trip, had prepared to lead a Youth With A Mission school for missionaries to Asia.

My Jonah Moment

A few nights before our departure, the house director decided to hold an all-night prayer meeting. Around two a.m., he began to prophesy over me, saying I should stay in Hollywood.

I was furious. *Who is he to say that to me?* I thought. *He's just trying to manipulate me into staying here.* I had my plans—I was going to Hawaii and would be a missionary to Asia.

Yet, despite my initial anger, his prophecy gnawed at me. Every time I prayed or thought about it, I couldn't shake the feeling that this might be what God wanted me to do. The struggle between my desires and what I sensed was God's leading became more intense, forcing me to confront whether I was genuinely open to His will, even if it didn't align with my plans.

Pushing all the thoughts and spiritual pressure aside, I decided to go home and make my decision far away from Hollywood. So, our team of five loaded into the old van and headed home. I was fleeing that place. I didn't like it anyway, and I wanted out. I told myself I was sick of people manipulating me and taking advantage of me, so off I fled.

We made it halfway through California before the old van broke down on an empty, lonely desert road. There was an abandoned gas station, so we parked there to wait for help. I walked out into the desert, feeling like Jonah, and screamed at Heaven: "I don't want to stay in Hollywood. I want to go to Asia. I miss my friends who are in Hawaii. Please don't make me stay in Hollywood."

I knew I could go wherever I wanted, but I kept feeling that unmistakable pull to stay in Hollywood. Once I got home, I decided to spend some serious time in prayer. I told God, "Now, no one's here to manipulate me. Please, Lord, help me hear Your call." And just like that, clarity hit me—I knew I had to return to Hollywood.

I remember picking up the phone to call my friend in Hawaii, bracing myself for his disappointment. But to my surprise, he said, "I think that's the right call." It's incredible how we can hear His voice when we truly listen. It is even more amazing how He confirms what He wants us to do in ways we don't expect.

Walking on water means following Jesus, not just carving your path. It's all about trust. I've realized that God's will is not just good—it's perfect. If I had gone to Hawaii, I would never have met my wife, Mary Jo, or come to Mexico. He was leading me all along; all I had to do was surrender and follow. The journey wasn't about where I wanted to go but where He called me to be, and that made all the difference.

Hollywood: The Sequel

I worked in Hollywood for two years and believed it would be my life calling. I ran a discipleship school for men all week, and on the weekends, I preached on the streets.

Back in the early eighties, Hollywood was a wild and dangerous place, full of sex workers, with Santa Monica Boulevard in West Hollywood being one of the hotspots. Every weekend, I focused on a few notorious blocks called "the meat rack." The sidewalks were crowded with young men who were available for purchase while johns (a name for men who pay for prostitution) drove by looking for a quick hookup.

I would lead teams out there to witness every Friday and Saturday night. Our starting point was Oki Dogs, a popular (and infamous) hot dog stand. The long lines of customers offered the perfect opportunity to share the gospel, initiating conversations with people who might not otherwise hear the good news.

The scene was intense, but that only made the work more urgent. It wasn't just about talking to people; it was about meeting them where they were, in the middle of their struggles, and offering a message of hope and transformation.

Date with a Drag Queen

I met Maria at Oki Dogs—she was a regular, always a familiar face in line. A young guy dressed as a young woman, totally bold and confident. Every time we crossed paths, I'd try to bring up Jesus. She usually just laughed it off or brushed me aside—until one night, something shifted.

I was walking behind her up the street, still trying to talk about Jesus, when she suddenly spun around and said, "You can come to my house."

I was stunned. That was not the response I expected. I knew I couldn't go alone, so I blurted out, "How about pizza tomorrow night instead?"

She gave a sly little smile. "Sure, it's a date."

As I walked back to Oki Dogs, it hit me: Did I just make a date with a drag queen?

The next day, I was borderline panicked. I ran to two of the girls on staff and begged, "You have to come with me tonight."

They shook their heads. "We've got a meeting. Planning stuff."

"I'll buy the pizza. Just have the meeting at the restaurant," I pleaded.

After some back and forth, they agreed.

That night, we showed up. Maria opened the door, totally glammed up—lashes, the whole look, beaming with excitement...until she saw I hadn't come alone. Her face dropped.

As soon as we arrived, the girls went to their table, and Maria and I ordered the pizza and then sat at a separate table. While ordering, the guy behind the register looked like he thought he knew what was going on. Maria, always the showman, winked and played along. But once we sat down, something shifted. The flirtatious vibe faded. Something real started to break through.

I invited her to share her story, which led to a heartbreaking truth. Her real name was Anthony. The childhood? Brutal—full of trauma and pain that were almost too much to take in. Locked in closets for days. Burn scars on the arms from a mother's iron. The abuse was relentless. Escape became the only option. Life on the streets turned into survival, no matter the cost.

I sat there, my heart heavy, trying to hold the weight of it all. And in that space, God's love rose up—not judgment, not condemnation—just love. Deep, unwavering love. I shared that Jesus had felt every wound, every loss. Nothing was hidden from Him, and He never turned away.

> In that space, God's love rose up—not judgment, not condemnation—just love.

For a moment, the walls began to crumble. The room grew quiet. A sense of surrender lingered—like maybe, just maybe, there was room for grace to break through.

Then the girls appeared.

"Our meeting's over," they said. "We have to head out."

In an instant, the moment vanished. The guard went back up. That familiar sparkle returned, but it wasn't real. The shield was back. The show resumed.

And just like that, the night was over. We went our separate ways.

That encounter wasn't random. It was a divine lesson in seeing people through the eyes of love. Jesus looks past the masks, the defenses, the brokenness. He sees the heart, the pain, the longing. "But when He saw the multitudes, He was moved with compassion for them, because they were weary and scattered, like sheep having no shepherd" (Matthew 9:36).

Another Scary Night

One night, as I walked back to the home I was leading from the office where we ran our twenty-four-hour hotline, I knew I was taking a risk. It was late, and this part of the city was nowhere to be alone. But before I could second-guess my decision, a young prostitute suddenly ran up to me, gripping my arm.

"Help me," she pleaded, her voice trembling.

I quickly noticed the blood trickling from a fresh cut on her arm, her dress torn and disheveled. She was shaking, eyes darting around in terror.

"He stabbed me," she kept sobbing. "Please, help me."

The urgency hit me like a jolt of electricity. She needed help—fast. Whoever had attacked her could still be lurking nearby.

I turned back toward the office, leading her through the dark streets of Hollywood. Every step felt like an eternity, my senses on high alert. Was he watching us? Following us? Would he come back to finish what he started? The moment's weight pressed down hard, but there was no turning back.

Finally, we reached the office. She was safe and able to get the medical attention she needed. I let out a breath I hadn't realized I was holding. Only then did I allow myself to think about my close call.

Later that night, as I finally made it home in one piece, I exhaled again, shaking my head at the absurdity of it all. Why do I always end up in situations like this?

Back then, I was pretty naïve and ignorant of how dangerous those streets were. But looking back, I see it clearly: the Lord upheld me through it all—every time.

Hollywood was a great training school for dancing on the water. Walking those streets and telling people about Jesus was risky, but the Lord held my hand through many dangers, toils, and snares.

48

CHAPTER 3
THE INVITATION

And Peter answered Him and said, "Lord, if it is You, command me to come to You on the water."
So He said, "Come."

Matthew 14:28-29

We often ask for orders, but Jesus extends an invitation instead. When Peter wanted to do what Jesus did, he asked for a command—but Jesus invited him to come.

Human nature craves commands, yet we fail to fulfill them. We like being told what to do because it allows us to rebel or be resentful—and even blame God when we don't follow through. This issue is at the core of what it means to walk by faith.

True faith requires us to trust Him and walk not by sight but from the heart. Commands, while necessary, can often stifle the heart's natural response. But an invitation—an invitation stirs something deeper within us, encouraging us to step out in faith because we want to, not because we have to.

I have been walking on water for over forty-five years. I know it sounds a bit extreme, but let me assure you it is true. Like Peter, I asked Him to command me, but He invited me to "come." I never knew where I would end up or how I would get there. I only heard His invitation and followed.

Although my call seemed to be to inner-city work and street preaching, it was never something I particularly enjoyed. Every day felt like a sacrifice. I plodded along, day after day, waiting for something to change. I believed that if you wanted to follow Jesus, you had to do whatever was most challenging and the most enormous sacrifice. As Jesus said, "He who finds his life will lose it, and he who loses his life for My sake will find it" (Matthew 10:39). I knew I had to lose my life.

All my missionary aspirations to go to Asia and work with like-minded people had to die. But I learned later that serving God isn't just about dying to self and sacrificing. It's about life—life more abundantly, joy unspeakable, and glorious.

I Was Never Enough

Before moving to Hollywood, I met a girl and spent a few days getting to know her parents in Northern California. It was an odd time. Whenever her parents saw us flirting or acting like a couple, they would pull her aside and rebuke her. The visit was an emotional rollercoaster, full of ups and downs.

At the end of the visit, I talked with her father. "My daughter is not the one for you," he told me, explaining that she was headed to nursing school and that I was an unacceptable match. He thought I was too young and not educated enough, and my past made me an inappropriate partner for his daughter. He then asked me to break off all communication with her.

Even though she was twenty-two, her father controlled her like she was still a child. I promised to wait for her and to respect his wishes. I wrote to him—not her—weekly for a year while I worked and stayed in Hollywood, trying to honor my commitment despite difficult circumstances.

After a year of faithful waiting, writing to her father, and praying, I received a letter from her.

Dear Dwight,

After much consideration and prayer, I have decided you are not qualified to be my boyfriend. You are not now, and you never will be. Please stop writing my father and waiting for me.

Sincerely, Elaine.

I was devastated. All my faithful waiting and planning had been for nothing. As the depression began to settle in, I knew I was in a bad state. The word "unqualified" kept running through my mind, echoing the feeling that I never measured up.

I started thinking about the friendships I had poured everything into, only to be rejected and "ditched" in the end. I was always the last pick for sports teams in school, a constant reminder that I never seemed to be anyone's first choice. The weight of these memories and the rejection made me feel small and insignificant, as if I would never be enough.

I remembered my kindergarten teacher, Mrs. Cook. I was utterly in love with her and hung on every word she said. One day, while playing with clay, I made a clay pizza for her. It was my way of showing how much I adored her. But while I was away getting a little carton of milk, my arch-nemesis, Carl, ruined my pizza and wrote on it, "Carl was here."

Furious, I acted impulsively. Just as Mrs. Cook approached, I threw the clay pizza at Carl. She caught me in the act, and to make matters worse, she held me tight as Carl pushed the ruined clay into my face. That moment, that humiliation, felt like the beginning of my disqualification, a moment that planted the seeds of feeling inadequate and unworthy.

My first friends and, eventually, my first girlfriends all rejected me. As a Christian adult man in ministry, those same painful feelings came rushing back.

At the time, I was running a halfway house with ten guys living there. All the guys started commenting on how depressed I seemed to be, and they said

I was a lousy leader. I couldn't even muster the confidence to talk with girls who would come around without becoming incredibly insecure.

Even though I continued to read the Bible and pray, it felt like God was on vacation. I kept going through the motions, hoping something would change, but deep down, I was convinced I was unqualified.

It went on like this for a couple of weeks until I opened my Bible one morning, and a verse leaped off the page: "Giving thanks to the Father who has qualified us to be partakers of the inheritance of the saints in the light" (Colossians 1:12).

"You may not qualify for them, but for Me, you are qualified," the Lord said. At that moment, everything changed. According to Jesus, I was as qualified as any other saint. Something deep inside of me shifted. Suddenly, it no longer mattered what people thought about me. I instantly became bolder and more secure. I could talk to girls without hesitation. I even found a newfound appreciation for Hollywood.

> "You may not qualify for them, but for Me, you are qualified,"

Jesus truly heals the brokenhearted. His words gave me the confidence and freedom I had longed for, and I finally understood that my worth came from Him alone. I was qualified in Jesus' eyes. His opinion counted more than anyone's opinion of me. The love of God casts out all fear, and when I understood His love, it cast out my insecurity and fear of rejection.

So This Is Mexico

"Will you please move to the base in the suburbs and lead the six-month discipleship training school?" the ministry director asked me. I was ecstatic. The idea of training other missionaries and traveling the world was thrilling. But then I thought, *You need to sacrifice and stay in Hollywood.*

After praying, I decided I could take a season to lead the school, but I knew I would have to return to Hollywood afterward. It was my cross to bear, and I accepted that calling with a sense of responsibility.

I moved to Lake View Terrace, a suburb nestled in the foothills of the San Fernando Valley. The students arrived in January 1983, and the adventures began. Each week, we hosted different teachers who brought a unique theme or topic essential for preparing the students for the mission field.

Our first school outreach took us to the Southwest U.S., eventually leading us to El Paso, Texas, and Juarez, Mexico. At the time, Juarez wasn't the best representation of Mexico. I remember the barren earth, the oppressive heat, and the many poor people we encountered.

One highlight of the trip was traveling four hours southwest to Ignacio Zaragoza, a small town in Chihuahua, Mexico. It was my first visit to a pueblo in Mexico, and I instantly fell in love with the people. Looking back, I realize that was my first authentic glimpse of Mexico.

Growing up, my perception of Mexico was shaped by stories of trips to Disneyland and Tijuana, where everyone returned with jumping beans, bullwhips, switchblades, and sombreros. Mexico never really appealed to me—I had my sights set on Asia, searching for someplace exotic. But the visit to Chihuahua changed everything for me.

After that trip, I began to see Mexico as a genuine mission field full of people with rich cultures and profound needs. It was a turning point that opened my eyes to a calling I hadn't expected.

Not All Callings are Crosses

When the six-month discipleship school ended, my great friend and my director, Ron, asked me to lead another one.

I told him, "I can't do it. I want to, but I must return to Hollywood."

He asked me why, and I replied, "Even though I want to lead another discipleship school, I have to go back to Hollywood because it is my cross to bear, even though I don't like it."

Ron looked at me and said something that hit me like a sack of bricks: "God doesn't always call you to do what you don't want to. God's will is good, acceptable, and perfect."

His words opened my eyes to the fact that even though the Lord tests our faith and commitment, He still wants the best for us. Serving the Lord is the most fulfilling thing we can do. It is a blast to do what He wants us to do.

> *Delight yourself also in the LORD,*
> *And He shall give you the desires of your heart."*
> *(Psalm 37:4)*

That moment reshaped my understanding of what it means to follow God. It's not just about sacrifice and struggle—it's also about joy, purpose, and the unexpected beauty found along the way.

So, I led the next discipleship school, which started in July 1983, and loved every minute. My friend Rod, a great musician, came on staff, and we led worship and composed music together. Later, we traveled around the Southwest of the USA and deep into Mexico together. We taught the students, played music, created dramas, and devised other creative ways to preach the gospel.

It Takes Two to Tango

A cute girl came to the discipleship school, but I had learned my lesson—I wasn't looking for a romantic relationship. After the six-month course had ended, that pretty girl, Mary Jo, came on staff. Soon enough, Rod, Mary Jo, and I became inseparable.

One day, as Mary Jo and I talked, I told her, "Hanging around you is like hanging around Rod." I meant it as a compliment, but she almost gave up on me right then. She still reminds me of that comment to this day.

One weekend during the third discipleship school I led, Mary Jo had to travel home. I didn't think much of it at first, but suddenly, I realized I missed Mary Jo. The thought hit me like a ton of bricks: *Oh no, I'm doing it again! I like Mary Jo.*

Determined to squash these feelings, I went for a walk in a nearby field, fully prepared to lay the relationship down and repent for liking her. But as I walked and prayed, a different thought from the Lord slipped into my mind: *What if it is My will?* It was as if God was gently nudging me to stop resisting and take a step forward to see how things might unfold.

As a single person, that's a rough lesson to learn. You can't force a relationship—it always takes two to tango. It will never develop if the other person isn't willing to take the same risk. But when two people hear the same call and decide to step out and walk on the water together, the dynamic is nothing short of incredible.

When Mary Jo returned, I was eager to see her but kept my feelings to myself. She could tell I was excited to see her, but neither of us said anything. There was a strange romantic tension in the air as I waited to make my move.

A few days later, we loaded the bus and headed to Mexico for a two-month trip. During our stops, where we served and preached the gospel, Mary Jo and I often walked together during our off-hours. We leaned into each other as we walked, laughing and talking like we'd known each other forever. But despite our easy connection, she couldn't help but wonder—what was I up to? Why hadn't I asked her to be my girlfriend?

Later, she asked why I didn't say anything about the relationship then. The truth was, I was waiting to call my friend and school director, Ron, to make sure it was okay that I dated her. I wanted to do things right, even if it meant holding back when everything in me wanted to move forward.

I Won't Be Your Girlfriend

We stopped in Mazatlán for a few days to rest and play at the beach. After setting up tents in a campground, Mary Jo and I went for a walk. A nearby hotel had a pay phone, so I had Mary Jo wait, and I called Ron.

"I LIKE MARY JO," I shouted over the poor connection. "I WANT TO ASK HER TO BE MY GIRLFRIEND."

"Go for it," is all Ron answered.

Of course, Mary Jo heard everything I shouted. We walked down to the beach and found a spot on a log, watching the waves crash against the shore. I could feel the anticipation building as I finally mustered up the nerve to ask, "Will you be my girlfriend?"

Mary Jo's response wasn't exactly what I'd hoped for: "No, I do not want a boyfriend." My heart sank momentarily, but she added, "I want to get married."

What started as a simple request to date suddenly turned into planning a wedding. It wasn't the expected response—it was even better. We decided to get married on December 15, 1984. The only problem was that the date was less than six weeks away.

> "No, I do not want a boyfriend."

"What do you mean the fifteenth? We've never even met Dwight!" my future father-in-law exclaimed over the phone to Mary Jo.

He was upset that his daughter was marrying someone he had never met. So, we loaded up my 1978 Toyota Corolla and drove from L.A. to San Jose, California, kissing the whole way.

"We approve of the wedding, but the fifteenth is too soon," my father-in-law said after we met in person.

So, I laid it all out for him. "Look, Mary Jo and I live on the same property, and we're always together. If we don't get married before January, we'll have to wait at least seven months—and let's be real, that's a long time to resist temptation."

He nodded, taking it all in. Then, without missing a beat, he said, "Ah, I see. I get it. It will be the 15th."

Just like that—problem solved.

At that time, I wasn't in a position to take on the responsibility of a family. I didn't have a steady income, and all I owned was a Toyota Corolla with 200,000 miles on it and a cheap guitar. Getting married felt like another step out onto the water. But we trusted that Jesus had called us to be together and knew He would uphold us.

> We weren't just called to walk together but to dance on the water together.

As I write this, we're about to celebrate our fortieth wedding anniversary, so I know we took the right step. The Lord even allowed us to honeymoon in Yosemite National Park, one of Mary Jo's favorite places. She is my soulmate, my inspiration, and my better half. We weren't just called to walk together but to dance on the water together.

Teaching and Learning

After our honeymoon, we dove back into leading the discipleship schools for the next three years. If you want to truly understand something, try teaching it. We hosted incredible teachers and studied missions, but most of our growth came from the experience of teaching others.

I was constantly challenged to learn how to lead people, guide worship, and deepen my relationship with God. Mary Jo and I also learned about each other, growing closer as a couple through each new experience. We faced challenging situations, witnessing firsthand how deeply life's struggles can mess people up. The students were great friends and honest servants of the Lord, but many carried heavy burdens and big problems.

Susan, a young woman we had helped escape a life of prostitution in Hollywood, joined one of our schools. She was determined to leave her past behind and grow as a new Christian. She had a little girl who had endured hell while her mother worked the streets. Every evening at eight p.m., like clockwork, the little girl would thrash and scream, her voice even dropping into a low, eerie tone like something out of a horror movie.

I knew it was a demon tormenting her, so with her mother's consent, we prayed fervently for deliverance, but nothing seemed to change. Night after night, for three long months, the little girl screamed and cried herself to sleep. It was heartbreaking to witness, and we kept praying for a breakthrough that seemed agonizingly slow in coming.

While on outreach, we stayed in an El Paso, Texas, church. The students spread out to use the Sunday School rooms as their bedrooms. At eight p.m. sharp, the familiar, blood-curdling screams pierced the air, sending a wave of dread through everyone. I remember silently praying, "Lord, why does this keep happening? What will it take for her to be set free?"

Then, a thought struck me: *It's her mother's fault.* I didn't want to add to Susan's guilt, so I wasn't about to tell her that. But then I realized this wasn't about blame but about belief. Susan believed that her daughter's torment was her fault, a direct punishment for her past life. Deep down, she felt she deserved the suffering.

I sat down with Susan once more to pray. "Do you believe God has forgiven you?" I asked her. "You have all authority as her mother and as a follower of Jesus. You must take authority and believe in your daughter's complete deliverance."

The fits stopped when Susan prayed with conviction and took authority over the situation. Her daughter became a delight to be around; her transformation was a testament to the power of God through faith and forgiveness.

Farther South

"We need to go farther south in Mexico," Ron told me one day. He explained how he had driven through a beautiful jungle area in Mexico on a trip to Guatemala and wanted to explore further. So, we packed up my trusty Toyota Corolla and set off.

This was 1985, before any four-lane highways on the west coast of Mexico. We drove straight to Mazatlán in twenty-four hours, navigating the narrow, winding roads that cut through the hills. It was the rainy season, and the journey's final stretch was a white-knuckle ride. Semi-trucks barreled down the road, crowding into our lane, and more than a few times, we were nearly pushed off the road. When we reached Mazatlán, I was sick from exhaustion and stress.

After some much-needed rest and recovery, Ron and I sat in our hotel room, praying for direction. "I had a vision of a green-pointed hill," I told Ron.

"I keep hearing Jesus calling us farther south," Ron said. So, we continued our journey southward.

As we drove through Nayarit, about three hours south of Mazatlán, something caught my eye—there it was, the green-pointed hill I had envisioned back in Mazatlán. It stood at the crossroads with another road leading to Tuxpan, a small town in Nayarit.

"That's the hill from my vision!" I shouted to Ron.

He then mentioned that he had contact with a local pastor, so we took the road to Tuxpan, feeling more confident than ever that we were on the right path. Eventually, we found the pastor, who lived in a small, one-room house with his wife and four children. It became clear that bringing a team to stay with him wasn't an option, and he didn't seem particularly interested in hosting us either.

So, we decided we would continue our journey south. However, while talking with the pastor, a young man approached us, eager to communicate but limited by the language barrier. Ron knew only a bit of Spanish; I didn't know a word. Despite the challenge, he insisted that we go to Rosamorada, a town we had passed a little way north.

The young man asked for a ride back to the crossroads where we planned to turn south, but when we got there, he refused to leave the car. "Go north. Rosamorada," he repeated, over and over, until we finally gave in and turned the car around, heading north toward Rosamorada.

In Rosamorada, we met Maria, who spoke perfect English and welcomed us to her small property. As she showed us around her modest home and yard, I couldn't help but think, *We could bring a team here.*

I asked her, "Do you want us to bring a team to visit and share the gospel?"

"That's what I've been praying for," she replied, her face lighting up with hope.

That's what it means to walk on the water—following Jesus as He invites us to take a step and trust Him to make the impossible possible.

Rosamorada became our project. We eventually bought land and built a small church there. The area was rough and hot, teeming with bugs and critters with a knack for biting and stinging.

I had no idea then that this simple step of faith would lead us to Tepic, the nearby state capital, and eventually to starting a thriving church in Tuxpan. It's incredible to look back and realize that all of this began with a simple vision of a green-pointed hill.

The Rough Trip Home

The drive back to Los Angeles was even more challenging than our journey to Mexico. After sixteen hours on the road, we desperately needed a resting place. I was delirious from endless driving, so we decided to stop when we spotted a rundown hotel around ten p.m.

The place was dirty and unsettling, with a massive guy behind the counter who looked like he'd stepped out of a horror movie. He offered to show us the room before we booked it, and we reluctantly followed him down a dim hallway. Bugs flew in every direction as he shut the window, making the place feel even more sinister.

When we entered the room, he disappeared around a corner to turn something on. Ron and I bolted for the car without a word, hearts pounding as we sped away. As we raced out of town, we laughed nervously at our escape.

"What was that?" Ron asked, wide-eyed.

"I don't know," I replied, still trying to catch my breath. "But I felt something evil in that place and just had to run."

Whether it was our exhaustion, paranoia, or something else, we knew one thing for sure—we had to keep driving to the next town. It was a close call, or at least it felt like one, and we were relieved to be back on the road, away from whatever spooked us.

> "I felt something evil in that place and just had to run."

Later that night, with Ron fast asleep beside me, I kept driving, desperate to find a place to stay. Around two a.m., I spotted a small hotel along the road and decided to stop. Not wanting to wake Ron, who spoke the most Spanish, I mustered up what little I knew and knocked on the door, hoping someone would answer. After what felt like forever, a tired-looking lady cracked the door open. I nervously blurted out, *"Dos personas."*

Surprisingly, she responded in perfect English, kindly informing me that no rooms were available. I thanked her and returned to the car, realizing we'd have to keep going. It was shaping into one of my life's most brutal all-night drives.

As I pressed on, the road seemed to stretch forever before me, and each mile was more grueling than the last. We encountered every imaginable hazard—wild animals darting across the road and drivers who seemed to have lost their minds. At times, my exhaustion blurred the line between reality and hallucination. I knew it was foolish and dangerous to keep driving, but the thought of stopping somewhere strange didn't sit right either.

Somehow, we made it through the night, our determination driving us as much as the car. Looking back, it was a miracle we made it home without stopping, and I've never been so relieved to see the familiar sights of home after that relentless journey.

I arrived very sick. I remember passing out in the bathroom from pure exhaustion. It took me a few weeks to recover, but it was worth it. We had a contact farther south in Mexico.

Accepting the Invitation Is a Lifestyle

Like Peter, Jesus invites us to come, and our faith response creates opportunities for God to do things we could not have imagined or planned. It's fantastic to experience—but also slightly terrifying at times.

I remember one incident toward the end of a mission trip in Mexico. We were returning to the border with a bus full of thirty-five students. As we neared the border, an unsettling pattern emerged—gas stations were empty, and no fuel was available. Our bus driver informed me with concern, "The bus's tank is big, but it won't make it much farther without refueling."

As he predicted, the bus sputtered to a stop as we rolled into the last gas station before the border. I thought we had narrowly escaped a disaster, but my relief was short-lived. The station attendant announced, "There's a gas strike nationwide. You won't find any gas."

I stared at him in disbelief, our situation sinking in. We were stranded in the desert with a bus full of students and no way to fuel up and continue the journey. It was one of those moments when we were forced to rely entirely on faith, knowing that only a miracle could get us out of our predicament.

The students started to complain, and the atmosphere became oppressive. They wanted to get home even more than I did. I went out to find shade behind some large gas tanks. "Why does this have to be so hard, Lord?" I asked. We were so close to home but stuck in the desert without gas.

> "Why does this have to be so hard, Lord?"

Then, when all hope seemed lost, two Green Angels appeared out of nowhere. Now, before you think I'm delusional, let me clarify. Mexico has a roadside service called the

Green Angels, a fleet of trucks patrolling highways to help stranded motorists with mechanical issues, fuel issues, and tire changes. However, they are few and far between. So when these two Green Angels pulled up beside us, I couldn't believe my eyes.

They saw our urgent need and immediately took charge of the situation. We had two twenty-gallon gas tanks on hand, so they graciously took me over the border, a half-hour drive away, so we could purchase enough gas to get us back on the road. With their help, we filled up and made it home safely.

Once again, the Lord had upheld us, providing a way out when the situation seemed impossible. The journey through the desert tested our faith and strengthened it.

God's invitations to walk and dance by faith kept coming, and with very little money, we made numerous trips to Mexico, the Southwest United States, and even Brazil during those years. Every trip was an adventure and a challenge with tremendous obstacles, but the Lord carried us through. Looking back, I realize we were walking on water—even when we didn't always recognize it.

CHAPTER 4
JUMP IN

Thus also faith by itself, if it does not have works, is dead.

James 2:17

At Youth With A Mission Los Angeles, we studied and taught about world missions nonstop. Every day was packed with ideas, classes, and endless discussions. But after a while, all the talking, planning, and theorizing drove me crazy. I wanted to jump up and shout, "Enough theory—let's do it already!"

We had spent months preparing, but I was done just thinking about it. I was ready to dive in, no matter the cost.

It was 1986, and I planned to take a team to Nayarit, Mexico. We would hike up the mountains to visit an indigenous community on the unreached people group list.

The trip finally happened in late March. We left L.A. before dawn with over thirty students packed into a school bus and a passenger van, ready for adventure and service. Our first stop was a church in Arizona where we could rest and prepare. In the church's gym, I couldn't resist climbing a rope. But in my enthusiasm, I felt a sharp pull in my back. Not great, I thought, but I pushed it aside.

The following day, we continued our journey to a church in Hermosillo, Sonora. Sleeping on the church floor was always uncomfortable, and the pain in my back made it worse. When I woke up, my back had had enough—it locked up completely.

While the students were serving Jesus passionately, reaching out to people, and serving the local church, I was laid out on my sleeping bag, flat on the floor, trying to get over the pain. I could hear life around me, but all I could do was repeat to myself, *Well, that's how it goes. You knew the price when you led the team, Dwight. Suck it up. You'll get better soon.*

After two days in bed, I felt well enough to continue our journey. We traveled to a small town in Sinaloa to visit our friend, Pastor Rocha. He opened his home for us, and we camped on his property. We used his outhouse, showered with a hose, and cooked our meals in the open air.

Evening in the small town was enchanting. We sat around a fire, drinking café con leche and bread, visiting and reflecting on the day's events. The food was delicious, and I still remember the smell of the wood fires. We enjoyed carne asada, grilled fish, roasted chicken, and pork everywhere we visited.

Mexican cooking is the best, especially when it is prepared by older ladies with much experience. There is nothing like it. Unfortunately, sometimes the hygiene suffers because of the heat, humidity, bugs, and a lack of refrigeration. It turned out that on this occasion, I ate something contaminated and got Moctezuma's revenge. We had a tight schedule and had to continue our trip, so we headed out the next day despite my aching bowels.

Our next stop was Mazatlán, Sinaloa, where we camped on the beach and showered in a trailer park. While everyone enjoyed the beach, I could not seem to improve physically. The temperature was scorching, and I was running a fever, so I needed a shady resting place. However, it was the week before Easter, or Holy Week, a vacation week for many people in Mexico. I walked down a secluded path, searching for shade, but people were everywhere. I would see a tree or shady area, only to find it already had people resting under the shade. I knew I had to be strong and pull it together, so I took some medication and went to sleep in the smoldering hot van. *Well, that's the way it goes. You knew the price when you led the team,* I thought again as I lay there sweating.

Finally, the day came for us to head south for Nayarit and our adventure to the indigenous people group. We drove to the small town of Rosamorada, Nayarit. On an earlier adventure, my friend Ron and I met a woman named Rosa, who had a home with enough room for us to camp out. She invited Mary Jo and me to stay in a room in her house while the students set up tents on her property.

Typhoid

As soon as we arrived, we set up the camp, digging a hole for the outhouse, setting four poles in the ground with a tarp around them and a hose over the top for a shower, and making a provisional kitchen with a tarp for a covering from the sun.

After we set up, I was exhausted, and my fever spiked. So, reluctantly, the following day, my wife and a team member took me to the bigger town nearby to see the doctor.

The doctor took a blood sample, and we received the results after a quick trip to the lab. I remember trying to read the results, but since they were all in Spanish, I could only recognize the word "normal." I thought I must be okay.

My heart sank when the doctor reviewed the results, and I saw the look on his face. "Tif-foi-dea," he said, shaking his head.

After some very slow translation on my part, it hit me: he was saying typhoid. *I have typhoid, and I am going to die,* I thought. I freaked out.

But the doctor calmed me down and made me understand it was not fatal. "You need to take the medication I give you and go on bed rest for ten days," he said.

So, I traveled over 1500 miles to rest in bed for ten days. *What a waste*, I told

> I have typhoid, and I am going to die.

myself. I had been so sick of sitting around talking, and now I was sitting around being sick. *Well, that's the way it goes. You knew the price when you led the team.*

Of course, it was not a Posturepedic, air-conditioned, comfortable bed rest. I lay on the floor in a small room with shutters for windows and the worst heat, humidity, and sewer odors I could imagine. If I opened the shutters, about ten local children would stare in at the crazy gringo that came all this way only to lay in bed. I could hear the rats running around in the ceiling and even see their tails hanging down from under curves in the roof tiles. The toilet was a hole in the ground, and I had to run past everyone in the camp whenever the diarrhea hit.

The medication was another problem. The doctor gave me four different pills. "Take one every four hours, one every six hours, one every eight hours, and one every twelve hours," he said. The problem was that whatever he gave me made me get high, so I couldn't keep track of when I took which pill.

The most challenging part of those ten days was hearing the remarkable stories from the students each evening. They shared their experiences and all the Lord was doing during their visit. I was happy that the Lord was using them and that they were having a great time, but I was frustrated with myself and the Lord. I felt useless. I did not want to waste this opportunity, but there was nothing I could do but lie there, try to sleep, and sweat.

> A filthy, scrambling rat had fallen from the ceiling and landed on my back.

We adjusted the plan so I could still go to the indigenous village after ten days of strict bed rest. *If I can get a good rest, I should be able to pull it off and maybe redeem this trip.* On the ninth night, I was determined—I had to sleep well. I knew that if I could manage a solid night's rest, I'd wake up rejuvenated and ready for the adventure ahead.

Have you ever gone to bed with that firm determination to sleep soundly, only to feel like you ruined it from the start? That was me. I lay down in my shorts, sprawled out on my stomach on the floor, with Mary Jo beside me. Sleep was just about to claim me when—suddenly—something landed square on my bare back.

These students! I thought in that split second. *They must be playing a prank. This is no time for jokes!* But whatever it was began to wiggle, and then it darted off me.

Instantly, I leaped up and switched on the light just as Mary Jo let out a blood-curdling scream. A filthy, scrambling rat had fallen from the ceiling and landed on my back. Without a second thought, Mary Jo bolted from the room, her shrieks echoing in the hallway.

Adrenaline surged through me as I entered full hunter-killer mode. I snatched up the nearest weapon—a flip-flop—and launched into action, my eyes locked on the scurrying menace. The rat darted and weaved, but I was relentless, pursuing it around the room with the zeal of a man possessed.

Finally, I cornered the vile creature. With a swift, decisive motion, I brought the flip-flop down, striking with all the force of my frustration. The rat twitched once, and then it was still.

Breathing heavily, I grabbed it by the tail, its lifeless body dangling as I strode to the door. Outside, the girls' screams pierced the night air, but I was unfazed. With a mighty swing, I hurled the rat into the neighbor's yard, watching as it sailed through the darkness.

Turning back toward the room, I declared with finality, "Now I am going to sleep."

We lay back down, and the day's exhaustion overtook me. I drifted asleep, only to be jolted awake by Mary Jo's voice, a whisper filled with tension. "Did you hear that? I think it's another rat."

My heart sank as I reluctantly got up and flicked on the light. The room was empty, with no rat in sight.

"Please, let me sleep. If I can get enough rest, I'll get better. Whatever you do, don't wake me up again," I begged, rolling over and desperately willing sleep to come.

With the meds and sickness weighing on me, I finally fell into a half-asleep mode. Then, something began to gnaw at the edges of my awareness. It was an irritating, unsettling feeling that my sick and half-asleep mind couldn't shake.

Though I didn't quite wake up at the irritation, Mary Jo was fully awake, listening intently. Someone was pacing around our camp, their voice cutting through the night as they yelled in Spanish. After what felt like an eternity, I vaguely heard Mary Jo's urgent whisper, breaking through my foggy mind. "Dwight, Dwight, someone is yelling."

I could not believe it. *What must I do to get a night's rest? God, do you hate me? Why are you torturing me? I just wanted one night's rest.*

Groggy and disoriented, I staggered outside to find a short, skinny man—reeking of alcohol—with a scruffy dog at his side. His clothes hung loosely on his frail frame, and his wild eyes darted about as he wandered around our camp, yelling incoherently about wanting a white girl. The night air was tense as all the students huddled in their tents, petrified by the unexpected intrusion.

I approached him cautiously, trying to gauge the situation. "Leave," I commanded him firmly in Spanish, but he ignored me, and his drunken rants continued relentlessly. For a moment, I got frustrated, but then it dawned on me that he was no real threat—just a pitiful, drunk, lost soul.

I grabbed him by the arm and led him up the road. *"Adiós,"* I said, releasing him into the night, hoping he would find his way home. Exhausted, I returned to the camp and, once again, announced to everyone that I was going to sleep and not to disturb me.

Finally, I collapsed into sleep, but when I woke on the tenth day, my body was as drained and sick as it had been on day one. The few hours of sleep I'd managed to snatch were nowhere near enough to get well.

As I lay there, the weight of disappointment crushed me. *Why did I even come on this stupid trip?* The question kept nagging at me, mocking me. I had set out to do something big for Jesus, but here I was—flat on my back, completely useless—while everyone else cared for me.

One Foot in Front of the Other

Despite exhaustion, we journeyed to the indigenous village on the tenth day. I didn't know if I had the strength to make it, but I held on to the promise from Deuteronomy 33:25: "As your days, so shall your strength be." With each step, I pushed myself forward, repeating that verse. The hike was grueling—a five-hour trek up the mountain and back—but whenever the thought of giving up crept in, I whispered to myself, "As your days, so is your strength; now walk."

The village was small, with just a handful of houses scattered across the rugged landscape, but the families received us with open hearts. We rejoiced as the families we visited welcomed the Lord into their lives. It was a moment of joy, a reminder of why we were there.

Then it hit me: *I have to walk back down the hill. I do not have the strength.* But I remembered the promise: "As your days, so shall your strength be." Based on that word, I put one foot in front of another and returned to Maria's house.

The next day, it was time to head back to LA, so we packed up and hit the road. On the journey, I informed our home base of my condition, and it wasn't long before they ordered us into quarantine upon our return, although I was no longer contagious and no one on the team got sick. Typhoid is passed through bad hygiene, so I never contaminated anyone. The reality of my situation hit me hard—I had contracted typhoid, and now, because of me, everyone else was being restricted.

Once we arrived home, I felt horrible, not just physically but emotionally. I couldn't shake the feeling that I had contributed little value to the mission. Instead of helping, I had become a burden. "What was that all about, Lord? I was trying to follow you and bring the gospel to Mexico, and it was like I had bad luck or something. Did I do something wrong?" I poured out my complaint to the Lord and waited for understanding.

In that quiet moment, I heard the Lord say, "Thank you."

I took all the pain and confusion and laid it down as an offering to the Lord. The Bible says, "And whatever you do in word or deed, do all in the name of the Lord Jesus, giving thanks to God the Father through Him" (Colossians 3:17). Everything we do is in His name—our lives are by Him and for Him.

Why do we go into the world? Is it just to help people and meet their needs? To feel accomplished and boost our self-worth? To gain wealth or influence? I had to ask myself these questions, and I realized—I didn't go on this trip for myself or to prove anything.

> I'm not concerned with applause from those still in the boat—I only want to please the One who called me.

When I heard "thank you" from the Lord, I knew it was worth it because I did it for Him.

The Bible reminds us, "And whatever you do, do it heartily, as to the Lord and not to men" (Colossians 3:23). That's the key. We can step out in faith because, in the end, it's all for His glory, not ours. I'm not concerned with applause from those still in the boat—I only want to please the One who called me.

The First Rat Story

One of my favorite Bible teachers came to our School of Evangelism in the early eighties. Sam Sasser, a missionary, told us the story of his work in the Marshal Islands:

> I wanted to go to the islands in the late fifties, but there were a few obstacles—mainly that they were being used as nuclear testing grounds. Oh, and pregnant women weren't allowed.
>
> My wife was six months pregnant, so I had to go alone. So, despite the risks, I took a leap of faith.
>
> When I arrived on my island, I found a hut to live in while beginning my work with the Marshallese community. It didn't take long to realize I wasn't the only occupant. The place crawled with giant rats—huge, fearless creatures that made themselves right at home. They nested in the thatched roof, their tails dangling over the walls like ugly decorations. I hated them. Whenever I spotted one with an exceptionally long tail, I made it my mission to take it out.

The work moved forward despite the rats, and people began to receive the Word over time. Then, one day, a letter arrived—it was permission for my wife and newborn son to join me on the island. I was overjoyed.

The day they arrived, I scrubbed the hut as best I could and hurried to the dock to welcome them. Seeing my wife and meeting my son for the first time was incredible. As a bonus, she brought a baseball and bat—maybe imagining a future where I'd play catch with our boy under the island sun.

We spent the afternoon settling in, then turned in early after her long journey. Just as I drifted off to sleep, I felt something land on me—a heavy thud on my chest. Before I could react, it scurried down my leg and, to my horror, bit off my big toenail.

That was it. The war with the rats had officially reached a breaking point. Fueled by rage and throbbing pain, I grabbed the bat my wife had brought and launched into a full-blown rat hunt, swinging wildly and chasing the little beast around the room.

Then I heard a small whimper.

I stopped mid-swing and turned to see my wife huddled in the corner, clutching our baby, staring at me like I had lost my mind. And at that moment—bat raised, toe bleeding, and a rat still on the loose—I couldn't blame her.

It took us some time to adjust, but eventually, things started to grow. In 1964, a revival broke out, sparking something bigger than I could have imagined. Today, thousands of Marshallese believers continue to love Jesus and "do the work of the ministry." Hundreds of pastors and leaders have been raised up, planting churches, discipling others, and spreading the Gospel across the islands.[1]

As Sam shared his story, something ignited in me—a deep, burning desire to follow Jesus wherever He led. I remember sinking to my knees on the classroom floor, surrendering everything, and praying, "Lord, let me serve You, no matter the cost."

We know challenges will come. Storms will rise, and trials will test us. But we also know this—He is with us on the waves, ready to catch us if we fall.

So go ahead and jump in without hesitation. No matter the threats of the enemy or the fears that try to hold you back, remember this: Jesus is already on the water, waiting for you. Don't stay in the boat. Step out in faith and follow Him wherever He leads. He will uphold you.

---

1 For more information about Sam Sasser, visit https://pacmiss.org/sam-sasser.

Divers or Toe Tippers

There are two types of swimmers: the divers and the toe-tippers. Toe-tippers linger at the water's edge, dipping a cautious toe to test it.

"It's too cold," they say. "It's murky; the current looks too strong."

Their excuses flow endlessly, keeping them on the shore, never fully experiencing the joy of the water. Meanwhile, the divers don't hesitate. With a bold leap, they plunge in, feeling the rush, embracing the experience, and living in the moment.

When God extends His invitation, our default reaction is often like the toe-tippers—hesitant and full of excuses. Our inner voices sound like lawyers. God speaks clearly and precisely, and we answer with a defense of excuses. "The water is too cold. I'll drown. Look at the wind. I can't speak well. I'm too young. I'm too old."

We are like Moses, who said to God, "Who am I that I should go to Pharaoh and that I should bring the children of Israel out of Egypt?" (Exodus 3:11). In this story, Moses gave God five excuses:

- I'm not adequate: "Who am I?" (Exodus 3:11)
- I don't know enough: "What is His name?" (Exodus 3:13)
- People won't take me seriously: "What if they won't believe me?" (Exodus 4:1)

- I am not good with words: "I have never been eloquent." (Exodus 4:10)
- I'm not willing: "Send someone else." (Exodus 4:13)

Any fool can find an excuse not to follow. Jesus tended to shut down the excuses instantly and bluntly. For example, He told one man, "Let the dead bury the dead" (Matthew 8:22 and Luke 9:60).

In John Bunyan's The Holy War, a cunning character named Ill-Pause is the devil's sly orator. Ill-Pause is right there whenever the devil speaks, whispering doubt and delay.

The author used this character as a metaphor to describe the subtle pause we sometimes take when the Lord invites us to step out on the water. Anyone who listens to Ill-Pause will never walk on water.

People often sit back, dreaming and fantasizing about the great things they will do for the Lord. They envision how incredible it will be to walk on water and do the impossible in His name. But instead of acting, they linger. They need more time to weigh the pros and cons and feel more ready and confident.

How many older people look back on their lives with regret, wishing they had responded when the Lord called? They remember when the invitation came but hesitated, and now they feel it's too late. They think they've aged out of their chance to make a difference. But here's the truth: We are never too old to walk on water—only too slow to respond.

When the wind is against us and the waves are roaring, it is easy to make excuses and stay in the boat. If we step out, we instinctively know there will be tests, temptations, and trials, but the one who walks by faith knows he is not alone in the water.

When you pass through the waters,
I will be with you;
And through the rivers,
they shall not overflow you.
(Isaiah 43:2)

CHAPTER 5
HE UPHOLDS US

"And He is the radiance of His glory and the exact representation of His nature and upholds all things by the word of His power" (NASB).
Hebrews 1:3

Just as molecules in solids are constantly vibrating yet held together by forces unseen, so too are we held together by something greater than ourselves. The realization that the Lord is the one who upholds us—every molecule, every breath, every moment—is essential for those who dance on water.

Each morning, I remind myself that keeping everything together is not up to me. When life feels like it could fall apart at any second, I remember that He is the one who holds me together. It's comforting to know that even when I'm at my lowest, it's not my strength but His word that sustains me.

I often say that Peter didn't just walk on water—he walked on the word "Come." Jesus' word defies gravity, and that small yet powerful word, "Come," kept Peter afloat as he stepped out in faith. This word reminds us of how crucial it is to understand our calling and recognize His invitation. We read in 2 Peter 1:10, "Therefore, brethren, be even more diligent to make your call and election sure, for if you do these things, you will never stumble."

Walking supernaturally requires knowing that you are called. It's His word that upholds you every single day. His word isn't just a spiritual concept—it's the force that holds together your bones, muscles, strength, and sanity.

If He doesn't breathe out, we don't breathe in. As the Bible says: "God...holds your breath in His hand and owns all your ways (Daniel 5:23). Being aware of His sustaining power is vital, trusting that He will keep us afloat and thriving, even during life's storms.

Sons and Daughters

We wanted to start a family while leading the missions school. But as time passed, it became painfully clear—we were struggling with infertility. For Mary Jo, becoming a mother was her deepest desire, yet month after month, that dream felt more and more out of reach.

We tried everything—doctors, treatments, medications—desperate for a breakthrough. But instead of hope, the medications only brought sickness, leaving Mary Jo feeling worse than before. Then, during a trip to Mexico, she fell seriously ill, and that was our breaking point. We made the difficult decision to stop the medications altogether.

Back in L.A., reality hit even harder. Funds were running low, and we could not pay the bills and medical bills with our income. Something had to change.

When the money runs out, it's a cue to ask God, "What's going on?" We've always believed that if God guides, He provides. But we found ourselves facing some hard decisions. I knew I needed to find some way to bring in more money if we were to continue with the infertility treatments. So, we made the tough choice to leave the ministry in Los Angeles. In 1987, we packed up our lives and moved in with Mary Jo's parents in San Jose, California. It was difficult, but we knew we had to trust God's plan, even when we couldn't see it ourselves.

> But we knew we had to trust God's plan, even when we couldn't see it ourselves.

Soon after moving to San Jose, I got caught up in the daily grind, working handyman jobs for my father-in-law. While it wasn't the life I had envisioned, I clung to the promise in Deuteronomy 8:18: "And you shall remember the Lord your God, for it is He who gives you power to get wealth." Remarkably, I started making more money than ever before, and soon, we were back in the doctor's office.

As I worked for my father-in-law and kept up with doctor's appointments, discouragement started creeping in. I felt out of place—no friends, no sense of purpose. The same old thought nagged at me: God is done using me.

Hoping to find a new direction, I applied for a college pastor position at the church where Mary Jo had first come to faith. But deep down, I felt out of my element. I even tried dressing the part—getting a sports coat and a fresh haircut—but nothing eased my insecurity. And when the church officially turned me down, it only confirmed what I feared.

"I am such a loser," I told Mary Jo as we sat in McDonald's one afternoon, frustration thick in my voice. "Everywhere I turn, I hit a brick wall. Everything feels impossible, like a dead end."

Without hesitation, she looked at me and said, "That's because you're not called to be a college pastor. You're a missionary. We need to go to Mexico and be missionaries."

Just like that, clarity hit. It was as if the fog lifted. We started making plans to move to Mexico as soon as possible.

Looking back, I still don't know where we got the certainty that God would make a way—but somehow, we just knew He would uphold us.

After numerous visits, the doctor called us both into his office. "After many tests and opinions, it is improbable that you will ever have children," he said. The doctor's words were like knives to our hearts. "You should seek other alternatives," he continued.

For Mary Jo, those words were devastating. Being a mother was her deepest desire, something she had longed for since she was a little girl. It was as if God had placed this dream in her heart, only to be crushed by circumstances beyond our control.

I tried to console myself by thinking that maybe I could be okay without children. We could travel more, focus on ministry, and have a different life. But for Mary Jo, the loss was immeasurable. The dream of motherhood was not just a wish—it was a calling, and hearing that it might never come to pass was like a piece of her heart being torn away.

A few weeks later, we traveled to Seattle to be ordained by our church. Surrounded by church elders who laid their hands on us, my heart pounded with anticipation. This wasn't just a formality—it was a prophetic moment, a presbytery, as it's often called, where we would be blessed and commissioned for ministry. I was eager to hear what God had in store.

The words spoken over us were powerful—full of promise, purpose, and the weight of divine calling. But then, one of the prophets began speaking, and what was said next caught me completely off guard.

"You will be a father and mother to many," he declared, repeating the phrase as if to drive the point home. "Your sons and daughters will come from afar, and your sons from the end of the earth."

His words echoed in my mind, and while everyone seemed to nod in agreement, I was fixated on what he was saying. Just a week before, the doctor had told us that having children was likely impossible. The disappointment was still fresh, and now here was this prophet, someone who didn't know our situation, confidently proclaiming that we would become parents.

> "You will be a father and mother to many."

This crazy prophet is off. He has no clue what he is saying, I thought to myself, struggling to reconcile his words with our harsh reality. But even as I doubted, a part of me wondered—could this be true? Could God be promising us something that seemed so impossible?

One particularly long day, my mother called out of the blue.

"Hi, Mom," I answered, surprised. She rarely called me—I was usually the one reaching out. "You know your sister is pregnant again, right?" she asked.

I did. My sister had been through a lot, married to someone battling addiction. Her twin boys had been born with developmental delays, and now, she was expecting her fourth child.

"She wants you to adopt the baby when he's born," my mother continued. "She knows she can't handle another child and believes this baby is meant for you."

Her call stunned me, and I instantly began to panic.

I struggled to find the right words. "Okay...let me talk to Mary Jo and pray," I finally said, still trying to process what had just happened.

We were still in the process of trying to get pregnant ourselves. We didn't have the money for an adoption and didn't live in Washington state, where the legal work would need to be done. You don't just adopt a baby. The word most prominent in my mind was impossible.

Then I told Mary Jo.

"Yay, a baby!" she shouted as she jumped around the room.

"Hold on," I cautioned her. "Don't get your hopes up. It's doubtful that we can even qualify, let alone pay for an adoption. First, I'll get some counsel."

Next, I called a pastor friend who had written a book about adoption.

> "It is impossible, and it never works, and you're not ready."

"Whatever you do, do not adopt someone from your family," he advised. "It is impossible, and it never works, and you're not ready."

Other close friends also urged me to be very careful. "What if the baby is born with developmental delays like her other children?" one lady asked.

Soon, we found out the gender: a boy. Mary Jo remained sure and confident that God was leading us to adopt him. I went out to pray, filled with doubt but willing to do whatever the Lord told me. As I walked and prayed, I had a conversation with God in my mind.

"How do you think this boy's home life will be if you don't adopt him?" I felt God ask. "Are you willing to take a risk?"

Hearing these thoughts, my only response was, "Yes, Lord." I knew He would uphold us by faith as we stepped out on the water.

Our first step was to move to my parents' house in Seattle. Adopting a child requires a social worker to conduct a home study and approve the adoption. We didn't own a home, have a steady monthly income, or have the funds to pay the social worker. We were the least qualified people to adopt a child. Throughout the process, we heard the word "impossible" too many times. All we could do was take it one step at a time.

Our assigned social worker was a lovely Christian lady who quickly became a great friend. She had no problem accepting my parent's home for the home study. "Don't worry about the costs," she said as we opened our hearts to her about our finances. She did not even have a problem with us taking the child out of the country three months after his birth as we planned to move to Mexico.

The birth was a dream come true. My sister gave birth and immediately handed Jesiah to Mary Jo. It was hard for her, as it would be for any mother, but she knew it was the right thing to do. She understood it was one of the most significant sacrifices she could make and never looked back. So much for the advice against adopting within the family! When it's God's plan, you can trust He will help you overcome all obstacles. God took care of the financial side of things, too. The birth cost was significantly less than it would have been if Mary Jo had given birth to the baby.

Three months after Jesiah was born, we moved with him to Mazatlán, Mexico (which I'll describe in more detail in the next chapter). Despite lacking the money, being unable to get pregnant, and not knowing how to raise a child, we were now on the mission field with a child. And we were on our way to seeing the crazy prophet's words come true. We had our first of many children, and we were parents. I can only say that Jesus upheld us through His word.

Another one

Mary Jo's itch for another child grew stronger as we settled into our life in Mazatlán, and less than two years into our time there, she began to express it more frequently.

"I want another baby. Maybe we can adopt here in Mexico," she would say, her voice tinged with hope.

However, the reality of adoption in Mexico during the 1980s was daunting. Adoption wasn't just frowned upon—it was met with outright suspicion. "Why did that mother abandon her baby?" was a common catchphrase and showed the deep-seated cultural bias against adoption. There were also rumors about foreigners—particularly Americans—stealing children, which only heightened the local mistrust.

Living in Mexico with an adopted Mexican child would have been incredibly difficult. The stigma of adopting a child would have compounded the prejudice we faced. It was a different time, and while things have changed since then—Mexico is now more open to adoption and mixed families—it was clear that adopting a Mexican child in the eighties was not a feasible option for us.

I repeatedly told her, "We've already received our miracle. You should be grateful for what we have and stop yearning for another child." We had several painful discussions, which often felt more like arguments. Eventually, I said I would only consider it if someone approached and asked us to adopt their child, but for now, she needed to let go of the idea.

A week after that discussion, I hosted a team from the USA. We set up in the town square near our house and invited people to our presentation.

Still mad at me, Mary Jo took our son for a walk in the stroller. At the last minute, she decided to head to the town square. Sitting on a bench, watching the team, she noticed a young, pregnant American girl whom she assumed was married to someone on the team.

To Mary Jo's surprise, the young woman, named Becky, came and sat beside her. They started a pleasant conversation, during which Mary Jo shared how Jesiah was born and adopted. After some time, Mary Jo headed home. Becky visited our house the following day and asked if she could speak with Mary Jo.

"I came from a Christian background and knew better," she said, "but I ended up in a relationship that led to an unplanned pregnancy. Now that I am turning my life around, I've decided to have my child adopted. Would you consider adopting her?"

That evening, Mary Jo cornered me. "You said that if someone came up to us and asked us to adopt their child, we could talk about it," Mary Jo reminded me.

What could I say? My own words had cornered me. I wanted another child, but the thought of actually making it happen felt overwhelming, almost impossible. The risks, the challenges, the uncertainty—I didn't want to set us up for heartbreak.

And then there were the obstacles. So many stood in the way that the practical side of me kept saying, *Be realistic. Don't get your hopes up.*

But you don't just adopt a child, especially while living in a foreign land. We did not have the funds or a home for the home study. Mary Jo jumped with joy while I trembled in fear and worry. I should have been more accustomed to facing impossible situations, but I still struggled.

The first challenge was finding a home in the US for the social worker's visit. By divine coincidence, Becky was from a town very close to my in-laws' new house in Santa Rosa, California, and her uncle was their pastor. This made my in-laws' home an ideal location.

The next hurdle was the financial aspect. We lived by faith, often struggling to make ends meet. The cost of traveling to California and staying there while maintaining our rented home in Mexico seemed far beyond our means. Despite the many miraculous provisions we had experienced, it felt like an insurmountable obstacle. I struggled with my doubts and fears as if I were faltering like Peter on the water.

All the same obstacles stood in our path as in the first adoption: no home, no money, no one encouraging us. It was even worse than when we had adopted Jesiah.

The number of enemies and obstacles that emerge while walking on the water is impressive. I was surprised by how many people criticized us and even became envious. "We have been trying to adopt for years. How come you guys have it so easy?" one person said. I asked a team for prayer for provision, and they accused me of trying to manipulate them for money. In retrospect, all these attacks were tests of faith like the wind. It was an attempt to discourage and make us sink, but God continued to uphold us.

We met the social worker who was assigned to us soon after our arrival. Like the social worker in our son's case, she was a Christian and happily accepted Mary Jo's parents' home for the home study. She even supported us monthly for years after the adoption.

Moving to my in-laws' house was not fun. We waited for my daughter to be born and listened to the endless doubts, concerns, and opinions of jealous and overly curious people. Becky, the birth mother, was committed to going through with the adoption, but a few family members pulled out all the stops trying to encourage her to keep the baby. When our daughter Rebecca was born, they insisted we wait a day before the birth mother handed her to Mary Jo.

> The number of enemies and obstacles that emerge while walking on the water is impressive.

The rule in California at the time was that adoptions were only final after six months had passed. If the birth mother had changed her mind, we would have to return our daughter. Amazingly, the State made an exception and let us take Rebecca to

Mexico when she was one month old. We spent the next six months fighting the fears and concerns that someone from her family would convince her to change her mind. Becky remained strong and kept her word to us. Later, she would have many children and even adopt. We returned after six months to finalize the adoption and marvel at the provision of God. He fulfills His promises.

Mountains moved with every step we took, and in the end, once again, the adoption cost us less than giving birth would have. No one can tell me that our abilities or wisdom made us a father and a mother. Jesus said, "Come," and He upheld us every step of the way. Being parents was impossible, but nothing is impossible for God.

Our children are living testimonies to the truth that God upholds us as we walk by faith. Over time, our family grew beyond what we could have imagined. Eventually, we established Nana's House orphanage, where children from all walks of life, from near and far, found a loving home. Through our work—starting churches and Nana's House—our family has expanded in ways only faith could have made possible. We've become a father and a mother to more children than we can count, fulfilling a calling that has touched countless lives.

With all its challenges and miracles, this journey is a testament to the incredible things that happen when you walk on the water by faith.

Eye has not seen, nor ear heard,
Nor have entered into the heart of man
The things which God has prepared for
those who love Him.
(1 Corinthians 2:9)

CHAPTER 6
MOVE EVERY OBSTACLE

"So Jesus said to them, "Because of your unbelief; for assuredly, I say to you, if you have faith as a mustard seed, you will say to this mountain, 'Move from here to there,' and it will move; and nothing will be impossible for you."

Matthew 17:20

As I gazed at the majestic Three Sisters Mountains in central Oregon, I thought, "What if I could cast one of them into the sea?" The absurdity of the idea struck me—imagine the outcry, the legal repercussions, the accusations of environmental destruction. But then I pondered: Did Jesus really mean for us to take this literally when He spoke of moving mountains by faith?

In biblical interpretation, metaphors like mountains are often understood figuratively. Jesus was talking about the seemingly impossible obstacles that stand in our way. When we speak His word in faith, those "mountains" move—not through physical might, but through the power of belief and trust in Him. Jesus spoke about the impossible and the obstacles we face as we walk in faith. We speak to our mountains by faith, and the mountains move.

The Numbers Don't Add Up

"The numbers just don't add up. We cannot move to Mexico with only four hundred dollars in monthly support. Our rent alone in Mazatlán is five hundred a month, and they plan to raise it by thirty percent in six months." I gritted my teeth as I tried to explain the impossible to Mary Jo.

It was 1988, and we had just moved to Mazatlán as full-time missionaries with a brand-new baby and no money. Mexico had strict rental laws that made it difficult for landlords to evict tenants who didn't pay, so nobody wanted to rent to the new gringo couple who couldn't even speak Spanish. This meant the only option within our reach was a scorpion-infested house that was still beyond our budget.

It seemed like an insurmountable obstacle, an immovable mountain—how could we make it even one month? But deep down, we knew we were following God's will. We stepped out in faith, trusting in the truth that where God guides, He provides. And every month, enough came in to cover the rent.

After a few months in Mexico, A pastor friend called. "I've got good news and bad news," the pastor said, his voice carrying a hint of tension. "Which do you want first?"

"Let's get the bad news out of the way," I replied, bracing myself.

"Well," he began, "we've been sending you ten percent of our church's income, but now we have to drop it to five percent. We're merging with another church, and they already support a missionary, so we have to split the support in half."

My heart sank, but before I could respond, he quickly added, "But here's the good news: once we merge, that five percent will be more than our current ten percent. You'll be getting at least twelve hundred dollars per month."

I was stunned. When I thought we were about to crash headfirst into a metaphorical mountain, God moved the mountain. It's always been this way for those who walk by faith—the Lord does the impossible when we walk in faith.

I often think about Peter in prison, on the brink of a dire outcome: "Now when Herod was about to bring him out, on that very night" (Acts 12:6 ESV). Why did God wait until the last possible moment to deliver Peter from decapitation? But then, I see how Peter had learned to dance on the water—he was sound asleep in that prison cell, entirely at peace. He had grown used to God's last-minute deliverances, so he rested in faith, unshaken by the threat.

> The Lord does the impossible when we walk in faith.

That first house in Mazatlán was such a test for us. Our son was at the crawling stage, and Mary Jo was constantly on edge, fearing the scorpions that seemed everywhere. People often tried to be encouraging by pointing out that a scorpion sting wouldn't kill adults—only little children. Naturally, that did nothing to alleviate our stress. Our son ate his first cockroach in that house despite her vigilance. I can only hope it was his last. We had to learn to trust God in those challenging moments, like Peter, resting in faith even when everything around us felt dangerous and uncertain.

The Language Mountain

Another mountain that had to move—although it moved much more slowly—was the language barrier. I was a twenty-eight-year-old American with minimal Spanish skills, so moving to Mexico took a lot of work. All I could confidently say in Spanish was, *¿Dónde está el baño?* But I was determined. "I will preach in Spanish within a year," I boldly declared to my friends.

To make that happen, I asked a young missionary, Dave, who spoke Spanish fluently, "Will you let me follow you around and help me learn Spanish?"

Dave agreed. I became his sidekick and chauffeur, since I had a car and he didn't. I started with a few grammar books but soon realized something crucial: language is more "caught than taught." Immersion was the key. As children learn through constant exposure and practice, I needed to use the language daily until I could speak it fluently.

Easier said than done. Despite all my efforts, I couldn't get the hang of it. Spanish seemed to have five to ten different words for the same thing, and its fourteen verb tenses were impossible for me to keep straight. It felt like my brain was just not wired to grasp the language. After a year of trying, I still wasn't ready to preach, so I decided to give myself another year.

I continued to throw myself into the language, reading the Bible aloud in Spanish daily, praying fervently for help: "Jesus, please give me Spanish." I clung to promises like Exodus 4:12: "Now therefore, go, and I will be with your mouth and teach you what you shall say," and Isaiah 51:16: "I have put My words in your mouth; I have covered you with the shadow of My hand."

After two years, I finally preached without a translator for the first time. Many people showed up, maybe to catch my bloopers, but it was a start. Today, Spanish is a significant part of my daily life, and I spend most of my time speaking it.

Border Trip from Hell

One of Mexico's unique features is that it borders the United States. While living in Mazatlán, we had to drive to the border every six months to renew our visas and vehicle permits. Each trip was a journey of faith, filled with challenges that required us to trust that the Lord would move mountains for us. In some cases, it felt more like entire mountain ranges.

One such trip was particularly memorable. My brother-in-law informed me they had purchased a bus for the short-term mission teams coming to Mazatlán for the summer. He asked if I could lead the summer teams and suggested that my sister and I head to Tucson, Arizona, to pick up the bus and buy everything we needed to host the teams.

When we arrived in Tucson, a local church generously allowed us to stay in some rooms next to their gymnasium. We spent a couple of nights there, and during that time, we filled the bus with everything we needed—furniture, a large refrigerator, kitchen supplies, and so much more. The bus was overflowing when we were ready to head back to Mazatlán.

We set out early the following day, driving an hour south to cross the border into Mexico. Customs was always a challenge, especially with our bus packed to the brim with supplies. As we watched others breeze through the "nothing to declare" line with similarly overloaded vehicles, we prayed for the same smooth passage.

When our turn came, the customs officer dropped a bombshell. "The president of Mexico just instituted a new rule: you cannot bring a passenger bus into Mexico without passengers," he informed us.

We tried to reason with him, explaining our situation, but he would not budge. Frustrated, we turned back to the U.S., feeling defeated.

But we weren't ready to give up. Nogales, Arizona, has two border crossings, so we decided to try the second one. After some tense moments and more negotiations, we were finally allowed through. However, our relief was short-lived. We knew that 32 kilometers into Mexico, we'd hit the interior checkpoint, notorious for turning people around or confiscating goods.

> "You cannot bring a passenger bus into Mexico without passengers."

We arrived at the 32-kilometer checkpoint, and our worst fears were confirmed when the official echoed the same line we had heard at the border: "You cannot bring a passenger bus into Mexico without passengers."

We spent the next hour pleading our case, trying every argument we could muster, but nothing seemed to move him.

"There's no way you're taking that bus into Mexico," he finally declared, walking away.

Frustrated and desperate, I turned to my sister and said, "Let's just sit here until a door opens."

The desert heat was relentless, and the bus turned into an oven as flies buzzed around us. Time crawled by, and just when I began to lose hope, I saw the official heading back toward us. My heart leaped, hoping he might have reconsidered.

But instead of the answer we prayed for, he barked, "Turn it around and get out of here. You cannot wait here any longer."

His tone left no room for negotiation. We felt like we had reached a dead end, with no option but to retreat. We turned around and returned to Tucson in shame and defeat.

Back at the gym, we huddled together, frantically brainstorming for a solution. The clock was ticking, and with a large team set to arrive in just a few days, the pressure was on. Out of nowhere, someone in Washington State offered to donate a Chevy Suburban and even to drive it to Tucson for us. It was a small glimmer of hope, especially since we already had one Suburban in Mazatlán, along with my trailer.

Two staff members drove our vehicle and trailer north from Mazatlán while we anxiously awaited the vehicle's arrival from Washington State. The green donated Suburban was on the way, and the two staff, Dave and John, showed up with our original white Suburban from Mazatlán. So, we made a decision. My sister and I would go first, and the two guys would follow in the green Suburban the next day.

"The starter was giving us trouble the whole drive up from Mazatlán," Dave informed us. "If you turn off the engine, it won't start again until the starter cools down."

We quickly repaired it; at least, that is what we thought. Then, we loaded as much as possible into the two Suburbans and the trailer. Unfortunately, we had to leave behind about half of what we wanted to carry, including the double refrigerator, but we managed to cram in a surprising amount.

With everything packed, my sister and I prepared for another attempt at crossing the border the following day, hoping things would go differently.

"You can't bring all this," the customs official said as we tried to cross again, but we persisted, and after two hours of arguing, we finally made it across and started our eighteen-hour drive south.

When we stopped for gas, the white Suburban would not start again. The starter was still acting up and refusing to cooperate. After a nerve-wracking wait to cool down, the engine finally sputtered back to life.

We continued our journey, and the pressure mounted. We had to be home in time to welcome the team arriving the next day, so stopping wasn't an option. But as the miles ticked by, the gas gauge slowly dipped toward empty again, and there was no avoiding it—we had to refuel.

I pulled into another station and told the attendant to fill it. He looked at me with a stern face. "You have to turn off the motor if you want gas," the old man said.

"I can't turn it off," I replied firmly, trying to keep my voice steady. "If I do, it won't start again."

"Then you can't get any gas," he shot back just as firmly.

So, I searched for another gas station, hoping this one would be different. I found one, but reaching it meant missing the entrance to the toll road, which was a faster and better-maintained route home. Instead, I had to stick to the slower, more dangerous free highway, winding through dust and heat mile after mile. The tension mounted with every bump and curve.

Eventually, I spotted the next entrance to the toll road and made a left turn, eager to get back on track. But in my haste, I missed the roundabout and made an illegal left turn, and before I knew it, the police were on me. They flagged me down, issued a ticket, and sent me on my way—another setback, another obstacle to overcome.

Back on the road, I noticed the engine starting to tick ominously. The sound was unmistakable: low oil. Without daring to turn off the engine, I pulled over, grabbed a couple of quarts, and poured them in, hoping this would solve the issue. The ticking stopped, and we were on the move again.

But relief was short-lived. Soon, I smelled burning oil and saw blue smoke rising from the engine. My heart sank as I realized what had happened—I had forgotten to replace the oil cap. The oil splattered out of the engine, hitting the hot exhaust and burning on contact.

> Everything that could go wrong went wrong on that journey.

We pulled over again, and I quickly poured more oil into the engine as my sister dashed to buy a new cap. Every minute felt like an hour as we struggled to get everything back in order. Finally, with the new cap secured and the oil level topped off, we continued our journey, battered but undeterred, determined to reach our destination.

We drove for hours until we eventually arrived at the last toll booth. I was so tired, dirty, and spent that I almost cried when the Suburban died there. We pushed it off to the side and tried to start it again, with no luck. Finally, I bought a bag of ice and pushed it against the starter to cool it off. To our immense relief, it started again.

We arrived home late that night, exhausted and frustrated with the Suburban. "Why is it so hard?" I asked the Lord. Everything that could go wrong went wrong on that journey. Little did I know that the summer's trials were not over yet.

Things Get Worse

Two days after our trip, we embarked on a four-hour journey south to Tepic with a team of forty people. We rented a small van and loaded the two Suburbans with staff and students. I was driving the white one that had given us so much trouble on the trip from the border.

Sure enough, about halfway to Tepic, the engine gave out. At that moment, I don't think I've ever loathed a vehicle more. It was then and there that I decided: I'm no mechanic, and from now on, I'll leave fixing cars to those with the patience for it!

The whole caravan stopped, and I had to evaluate our situation. How could I get the forty-plus-person group to town? After some thought, I asked all of them to cram into our remaining vehicles—a van and the green Suburban—which technically only seated twenty-three.

We arrived at a small church in Tepic, unaware that this place would become a significant part of our lives. After the exhausting trip filled with one obstacle after another, I was utterly drained, and I faced the challenge of finding another way for the rest of the team to return since I couldn't ask forty-something people to squeeze back into two vehicles for the entire ride home.

While the team ministered and God moved powerfully, I found myself retreating behind the church, overwhelmed with emotion. I wept, asking the Lord, "What am I doing wrong? What are You trying to teach me? Can I quit? Please, choose someone else to lead these teams."

After pouring out my heart, I pulled myself together. Despite only having two hours of sleep, I got a good portion of the team onto a four-hour bus ride to Mazatlán. I sent a tow truck to get the broken-down Suburban and drove back home to prepare for an even larger team that arrived in two weeks.

It was raining steadily the night before the new team arrived. I was working on my Atari 520-ST in the quiet of my home office when Mary Jo shouted, "The car is underwater!"

My heart skipped a beat. "What?" I gasped, my mind reeling. "You've got to be kidding!" Panic gripped me as I sprinted outside to rescue my Chevy Blazer.

Her words were no exaggeration. We had recently moved into a new rental house and were unaware that our street was susceptible to annual flooding—a harsh lesson we learned that day. The torrential waters had completely submerged my truck, my sister's Jeep, two Chevy Suburbans (including the one that blew its engine on the way to Tepic and which we had painstakingly rebuilt), and even the bus a mission team had just brought down. These vehicles, parked in anticipation of the arrival of a mission team with over

> "The car is underwater!"

a hundred students, now sat helplessly submerged in floodwaters on the road beside our house.

With adrenaline coursing through my veins, I tried to maneuver my truck to higher ground, but it sputtered and stalled as I attempted to back up. Soaked to the bone and overwhelmed by frustration, I crushed my finger in the gate while trying to rescue more vehicles from the rising tide. Yet, despite my frantic efforts, the inevitable happened: everything was flooded. Each engine, transmission, and fuel tank was submerged, requiring a complete change of oils and fluids for every affected vehicle.

For the next ten days, as the smelly water receded, I found myself in a relentless whirlwind of activity, scarcely allowing myself the luxury of sleep as I juggled countless tasks to ensure the success of the visiting team's mission. I ran between tasks and hardly slept for most of that team's ten-day visit, but we made it through.

Honestly, the entire summer of 1990 was relentless. Obstacles blocked my every move, and I couldn't understand why everything was so difficult.

After our busy summer season of mission teams, Mary Jo flew to the USA to visit her parents, and I set off to meet her in San Jose, California, in my newly repaired Blazer. The drive went smoothly, and I enjoyed myself. I was determined to set a new personal record on the drive north.

However, just outside Obregon, Sonora, I noticed traffic had reached a complete standstill.

Curious, I approached the driver in front of me and asked, "Why is everyone stopped?"

He replied, "There was a flood two days ago. The road ahead is six feet underwater. We've been waiting on the road for two days."

I grabbed my Bible and went to the back of my Blazer, deciding to use the unexpected downtime to pray. After about an hour, I thought, *Why not head back into town and find a hotel?*

Though most of the hotels were nearly at full occupancy, I managed to find a room, enjoy a satisfying meal, and get a good night's rest. The following day, I switched on the TV, and the first thing I heard was the announcer reporting that the road had been cleared. I returned to the highway calmly and continued my journey to San Jose, CA.

As I drove, I realized that something had fundamentally changed within me. I didn't panic over the flood or the road closure. I didn't feel the familiar stress that would have usually taken over. There was no more questioning God or asking why things were going wrong or what I had done to deserve this. Instead, I felt an unexpected sense of peace.

> I now refer to that challenging summer as my "training in patience."

Looking back on that experience, I now refer to that challenging summer as my "training in patience."

We say, "Lord, give me patience right now." But patience takes time and trials to learn. "My brethren, count it all joy when you fall into various trials, knowing that the testing of your faith produces patience" (James 1:2-3). When Jesus told His disciples that mountains would be cast into the sea, He didn't give them a time frame. Often, we expect mountain-moving to be instantaneous, but I've learned the hard way that some hills are stubborn and slow. In those moments, our patience is proof of our faith.

Held Together by Grease and Faith

"What do you need most?" a pastor asked me on a trip to Seattle in 1993.

Without hesitation, I answered, "A reliable vehicle."

At the time, I would drive up the West Coast of America from central Mexico several times a year, and it was a challenging journey. My old gas-guzzling Ford Bronco, which I upgraded from the Chevy Blazer, was too unreliable and dangerous for my family to travel such long distances. The mountain in our way was the money needed to get something better.

All the pastor said was, "Okay." But in the next church service, he stood and declared, "We are going to buy Dwight a new vehicle. Who wants to give?"

The church members came forward and gave seventeen thousand dollars. Then, another member mentioned he had a contact at the local Ford dealership. By the next day, our mountain was moved, and I signed a contract for a brand-new Ford pickup.

It was a huge miracle, but one last obstacle remained: I had to get my old Bronco from Mazatlán, Mexico, to Seattle, Washington, to trade it in. After returning to Mexico, I grabbed a close friend named Javier, and together we set off. We drove relentlessly through the deserts of northwestern Mexico and the southwestern United States, making it to Los Angeles in two days. With a tight deadline to reach Seattle by Sunday, we pushed ourselves to keep going.

However, as we approached the mountains of northern California, we hit snow, and the winding, icy roads slowed our progress. Javier looked at me wide-eyed and pleaded, "I've never seen snow before. Can we stop? I want to touch it."

Reluctantly, I took the exit for the small town of Shasta. Fortunately, the road sloped uphill because the truck continued rolling when I applied the brake. Using the emergency brake, I halted on the shoulder and got out to investigate what was wrong.

Everything looked okay until I saw the passenger-side front tire hanging at a 45-degree angle. The bearing housing had broken off, and the disk brake pads were gone. It was a miracle that the wheel didn't fly off on one of the curves. Thank God Javier wanted to touch the snow.

The problem was that it was a weekend in a small town, and we needed to be in Seattle by the following day, a ten-hour drive away. I needed all new parts for my front wheel, and I needed them quickly. We found an open auto parts store with the new bearing and brake parts. However, they didn't have the bearing housing, which was only available at a junkyard.

Taking all the parts and a lot of grease, I put everything back together, stuffing it with grease and wrapping plastic around the exposed part.

Soon, we were on the road again. The wheel wobbled, and Javier had to look out the window every few minutes to check it. By the time we reached Seattle, he had seen more than enough snow.

> It was the hand of God that held us—and that Bronco—together.

The following Monday, we went to the dealership to pick up the new truck and trade in the old Bronco. Just as we pulled into the lot, the brakes went out again. That truck miraculously held together until the last second.

It was the hand of God that held us—and that Bronco—together. I know He sustained me once again as we stepped out in faith. He moved all obstacles to get us the vehicle we needed to do His will in Mexico.

Overcoming Your Mental Mountains

Some mountains are in your mind. You have a concept or limitation that you learned to live with, but you need to overcome it and move the mountain by faith.

"Dwight, don't get me wrong, but you're not a primary leader, and you're not administrative," an older businessman and leader told me in 1991 when I inquired about possibly directing a Youth with a Mission center in another city in Mexico. "You don't have what we need, but you can help the guy we're sending."

I can't even begin to count how many times people have labeled me or told me I wasn't good enough. "You're such a clown. You don't have a degree. You're not cool. You're disorganized." Over and over, people cast their judgments, telling me what I couldn't be.

But Jesus finally broke through to me. He said, "I don't want you to live by other people's words; I want you to follow Me. I will move every mountain, every obstacle in your way."

People quickly label you based on your failures or perceived inadequacies, even turning them into stumbling blocks. But I learned not to let others define me. Their opinions don't dictate my worth or my path.

It does not matter if you are incapable, not smart enough, or if it is not your gift. All that matters is if He said, "Come." God always calls you to do the impossible, to move mountains. I imagine people standing and mocking you as you speak to your mountains. Always remember that they do not have the same calling as you. They have their mountains and do not have the grace for yours.

As a brand-new Christian, I was fortunate to know several older church members, but one woman in particular became a true mentor to me. She gifted me a Bible, and on the inside cover, she wrote Isaiah 45:2–3:

> *I will go before you*
> *And make the crooked places straight;*
> *I will break in pieces the gates of bronze*
> *And cut the bars of iron.*
> *I will give you the treasures of darkness*
> *And hidden riches of secret places,*
> *That you may know that I, the* Lord,
> *Who call you by your name,*
> *Am the God of Israel.*

Those words have stayed with me ever since. Whenever I encounter "gates of bronze" or "bars of iron," I lean on this promise. I know the God who moves mountains. For Him, nothing is impossible. When people say I can't do something Jesus has called me to, I follow His word, not theirs.

When someone tells you that you can't do something, look to Jesus. If He says, "Come," step out and obey. Do it, even if they mock you and tell you how impossible it is.

That's how you begin to walk in faith. And if you keep walking long enough, you'll find yourself dancing on the water.

CHAPTER 7
KEEP LOOKING AT JESUS

If then you were raised with Christ, seek those things which are above, where Christ is, sitting at the right hand of God.

Colossians 3:1

We used to sing a little song:

> *Peter tried to walk on water,*
> *But things kept getting harder, harder.*
> *He looked down, and then he took a bath.*
> *Now, the moral of this story is,*
> *Don't look down when you're bound for glory;*
> *Don't look down on your dirty, rotten past.*

It's a simple song, even a silly one, but it makes an important point: what you focus on matters. When you're walking on water, you can't afford to be distracted by the wind and the waves. The only way to do that is by intentionally focusing on Jesus.

I'm reminded of the story of Nehemiah, who was appointed governor over the exiles who returned from Babylon to rebuild Jerusalem. Despite facing overwhelming obstacles, he remained focused on his mission. His enemies tried every possible tactic to distract him and stop the reconstruction of the city's walls. Nehemiah wrote about one of his enemies: "For this reason he was hired, that I should be afraid and act that way and sin, so that they might have cause for an evil report, that they might reproach me" (Nehemiah 6:13).

I often reflect on Nehemiah's perseverance during challenging times. The enemy loves to sow distractions, detonating metaphorical bombs around us to stir fear and distract us from God's purpose. The key to victory is to keep our eyes fixed on Jesus, even when things around us are chaotic, confusing, or even contradictory.

Can't Wear Me Down

I first understood this principle many years ago when I was single and somewhat stupid. (Maybe "innocent" is a better word, but stupid is how I felt sometimes!) Anyway, I was a relatively new Christian and was friends with a girl, and she had a roommate I was attracted to. I had asked my friend if I could visit her and her roommate sometime in their small apartment, and she agreed. Unbeknownst to me, my friend had had feelings for me.

When I arrived, my friend met me at the door and said, "I don't feel well; I have a cold."

Concerned, I offered to take her to a restaurant, thinking it might cheer her up. But she declined, saying, "I'm sorry. I feel awful. Maybe another time."

Not wanting the visit to go to waste, I asked her roommate, who I was attracted to, if she wanted to go out instead. She agreed, and we had a great time together, leaving me hopeful that something more might develop between us. However, when we returned, my friend pulled me aside and asked if we could talk.

"That was so mean! Why did you come to see me and then go out with her?" she demanded, visibly furious.

I was taken aback and immediately apologized, asking her to forgive me for being so insensitive, but she wasn't finished. Her rebuke continued, concluding with the comment, "You need inner healing."

I left feeling destroyed and depressed, and from that point, I began to dig up every fault and failure I could find in myself. The more I examined, the worse I felt.

It wasn't long before others started noticing my gloomy mood. "You're supposed to be the leader," they'd say. "Why are you moping around? Where's the joy of the Lord?"

Everywhere I turned, someone seemed to have a rebuke waiting for me. Between the emotional turmoil and a full workload, I was wearing thin. Then I came across a verse in Daniel 7:25: "He will speak out against the Most High and wear down the saints of the Highest One" (NASB). Then it struck me: The devil is wearing me down, I thought.

In my early twenties, I was already burned out. I had heard stories of ministers who didn't last in ministry because of burnout, and I wondered if that was my fate, too.

Fortunately, I received some time off, so I went to Washington to visit home and meet with my pastor. "The devil is burning me out," I told him. I confessed that I needed inner healing and felt like a complete failure, even quoting the verse from Daniel. "I think I'm burned out," I added, feeling utterly defeated.

"Dwight, you have your eyes on the devil. You need to keep your eyes on Jesus," he said. "Don't focus on what the devil is doing or your failures. Look at Jesus. He is the Author and Finisher of our faith."

Of course, he was right. What was I thinking? Like Peter, I had been looking at the wind and the waves, letting fear and doubt consume me. The words of the old chorus by Helen H. Lemmel came to mind:

> *Turn your eyes upon Jesus,*
> *Look full in His wonderful face,*
> *And the things of earth will grow strangely dim,*
> *In the light of His glory and grace.*[2]

---

2 Helen H. Lemmel, *Turn Your Eyes Upon Jesus* (1918).

As soon as I looked at Jesus again, by faith, my heaviness and oppression lifted. I did not need inner healing because my old self was crucified with Christ. The devil could not wear me down because the Lord was my strength. I was back to walking on the water because what was impossible for me was possible for Christ.

I wish I could say that was the last time I ever took my eyes off Jesus, but I can't. What I can say is that the lesson I understood then has stayed with me to this day. When I feel myself spiraling into fear, shame, or insecurity, I have learned to move my focus off of myself—my weaknesses or problems—and onto Jesus. When storms rage and wind blows, that's the only way to stay above water.

The Secret Life of a Shrimp Seller

This principle of focusing on Jesus is essential not only when we can see our enemies around us but also when we are navigating unseen, unknown dangers.

A couple of years after moving to Mazatlán, when I first began ministering in the mountains of Sinaloa, I wanted to blend in with the locals. It wasn't until later that I realized I was in an area where drug lords grew the drugs they sold. Initially, I was unaware of the extent of the drug trafficking in the region. I would boldly drive into town and start talking to people about Jesus. But I quickly noticed that people were highly resistant to me—many avoided me, and no one would invite me into their homes.

My first real friend in town was El Gallo. He liked teasing me as I sat at his little shrimp cocktail stand in the town center. "Why are you here?" he would ask. "Are you looking for a girl, drugs, or money?"

"No," I would reply. "I'm here to invite you to know Jesus and come to church with me."

Our conversations were always the same, but little by little, he warmed up to me. Eventually, he even helped me find a place to rent—something no one else would do for me.

One day, El Gallo confided, "Everyone in town thinks you're a DEA agent. Nobody believes all that Jesus stuff you're talking about, and no one trusts you. When people see you coming, they run to hide their pot plants."

"Oops, I had no idea," I told him, assuring him I wasn't part of the DEA.

El Gallo helped me, but he had some problems and was connected to the drug trade. I always wondered how a simple shrimp cocktail cook could make so much money and have so much.

One day, El Gallo announced he was heading into town. "Can I get a ride?" a young man asked, and El Gallo quickly agreed. On the road to Mazatlán, some men pulled them over and shot El Gallo in the face seven times. The young man who had asked for a ride tried to flee, but they shot him in the back.

It wasn't until after this tragedy that I learned El Gallo was a money launderer who had crossed the wrong people. I would have been more cautious about spending time around him if I had known—but I didn't know.

While it's wise to avoid danger when we can, there are times when we're unaware and find ourselves walking through dangerous places. The only truly safe place is in God's will, with our eyes fixed on Jesus—not on the distractions around us.

The Lord Will Catch You

My sister and her children, who also lived in Mazatlán, visited one day. While Mary Jo and my sister were chatting, the children played outside. The neighbors had hung a swing from a tree on the small island that divided the road in our quiet residential neighborhood.

Suddenly, a loud crash startled my wife and sister. They ran outside and saw Levi, my sister's son, face down in the road. Two cars had just passed by as he ran toward the swing. The slower car had hit him, sending him flying and flipping some distance, while the faster one sped off without stopping.

Fearing the worst, they rushed to him. To their immense relief, he seemed fine, apart from a bump on his head and a small cut. The man who had hit him took full responsibility and insisted on taking Levi to a doctor. Amazingly, Levi didn't have a single scratch beyond the minor bump.

"What happened?" my sister asked Levi.

He replied, "That man caught me."

But no one else was on the road, and the other kids saw him alone. We concluded that an angel must have caught him, and the Lord had protected his life.

I love the verse, "The eternal God is your refuge, and underneath are the everlasting arms" (Deuteronomy 33:27). I often remind myself that the everlasting arms are always there to catch me. How many times does the Lord see us when we're entirely unaware? Those who walk by faith are attuned to the unseen realm—they know the Lord has given His angels charge over them.

> How many times does the Lord see us when we're entirely unaware?

We witnessed the Lord's protection and provision many times in Mazatlán. As we kept our eyes on Jesus, He safeguarded us and met our needs. Even when the rent was about to go up, we found a cheaper, safer place in a much better location—His hand was on us every step of the way.

They Stole Everything

The church's front door wasn't just open—it was lying on the ground, smashed off its hinges. As Dave and I stepped inside, we were hit with what had happened. Everything had been stolen: our new thousand-dollar keyboard, sound equipment, computers, cash, and several instruments.

I was overwhelmed with a deep sense of discouragement and violation. We had scraped together every bit of funding to acquire that special equipment for the church in Mazatlán, and now it was all gone.

Two neighbors approached us, saying, "We know who broke in. It was the kids who live on the next street." It was a gang, a dangerous group we were well aware of.

Rather than giving in to the despair and anger that were trying to control our reactions, we took a few moments to pray together in the middle of our ransacked office. We asked God for His peace and direction and contacted the police.

"We know who did it. Can you please go and retrieve our things?" I asked the two police officers who had responded to the break-in.

"We will try to look into this," they replied, their tone noncommittal.

That's when it hit me: these guys earned around five dollars daily. There was no way they would risk confronting a gang for nothing. "I'll give you four hundred dollars each if you recover our things," I offered.

They contacted me by the afternoon. "We have your things. You can come pick them up," they said.

When I arrived at the station, I saw they had recovered about half of our stolen items. I handed each of them two hundred dollars.

"You said four hundred," they reminded me.

"Yes, for all our stuff, but this is only half," I replied.

By the evening, they called again, with the remaining items—everything except a computer drive worth about a hundred dollars. Ultimately, it cost me eight hundred dollars, but we recovered items valued at several thousand dollars.

This situation reminded me of the Bible story when everything was stolen from David and his men, including their families. The men, devastated by their loss, even considered killing David. But instead of giving in to despair, David turned his eyes to the Lord:

> *Now David was greatly distressed, for the people spoke of stoning him because the soul of all the people was grieved, every man for his sons and his daughters. But David strengthened himself in the Lord his God. (1 Samuel 30:6)*

Even in tragedy and loss—or especially in tragedy and loss—we must always look to Jesus. The wind may blow, and the waves may rise, but if we keep our eyes on Him, He will keep us above the storm, and we'll come out on the other side.

San Ignacio

In 1993, I knelt in the dirt on the road in front of the little house we rented in San Ignacio, Sinaloa. Every Sunday, we made the hour-and-a-half drive from Mazatlán to this small pueblo, deep within a notorious drug-trafficking region. We had saturated San Ignacio for over two years with Bibles, special events, visitations, prayers, and tracts. But that day, no one came to the service after all the preparation, countless practices, and setting up chairs and sound equipment.

As I knelt there, frustration overwhelmed me. I felt an urge to curse the town, to shake the dust from my feet, and leave it all behind. *Life was much easier before I decided to come here,* I thought. *They don't want me here, and I'm just casting my pearls before swine.*

In that moment of discouragement, I prayed for patience, struggling to find purpose amidst the rejection. Then, the Lord reminded me of a promise He had once given me: "For I am with you, and no one will attack you to hurt you; for I have many people in this city" (Acts 18:10).

I chose to believe in His promise, and when I looked up, a few people had arrived. We ended up having an excellent church service, and once again, the Lord encouraged us.

We worked in San Ignacio for five years, each step feeling like a struggle. Unbeknownst to us, at first, we had started the church in the house of a known drug lord. On the very road where we rented that house, every neighbor had lost someone to violence. One young man from our church was traveling through the mountains on his mule when he stopped to help someone with their horse; they shot him in cold blood.

> The only reason we're still here is that we refused to leave.

I wanted to quit countless times. The town felt impossible to reach, and I often dreamed of moving on to other ministry opportunities. But I could never shake the words Jesus had given me: "I have many people in this town."

People of faith don't shrink back. The only reason we're still here is that we refused to leave. We don't look back at the boat we stepped out of, and we don't look down at the waves beneath our feet. We keep looking at Jesus.

If you wish you were somewhere else or someone else, you may need to look at what you are focused on. Are you focused on what you have or what you don't have? It is a lie to think you will change if you change location or vocation because wherever you go, *you* will be there. The Bible says:

> *Now the just shall live by faith;*
> *But if anyone draws back,*
> *My soul has no pleasure in him.*
> *But we are not of those who draw back to perdition, but of those who believe to the saving of the soul."*
> *(Hebrews 10:38–39)*

When you focus on Jesus, you find the strength to persevere even when storms last much longer than expected. How often do we give up just before the clouds break and the sea calms? While it's tempting to focus on the challenges, disappointments, and dangers that surround us, if you can turn your eyes to Jesus, you'll find the strength and endurance to finish God's calling.

Stupid Ear, Stupid Nose

Eventually, the Lord spoke to my heart, saying, "It's time to start in a new town." After five years in San Ignacio, the church was small but stable. I knew it was time for a new step. We had a pastor prepared to stay behind and continue the work, but the mission team from Mazatlán needed to move forward. I gathered the team and shared my conviction: it was time to start a church in another town.

Our team had grown to love San Ignacio, but I felt sure. "We have to step out. We'll never move forward unless we walk in faith," I said as I conveyed the vision that had been placed in my heart. Each team member understood, and we prepared to take that next step of faith together.

We launched the church in La Cruz, Sinaloa, with a special event in the town square. Unlike San Ignacio, the people in La Cruz were hungry for God. Hundreds turned out for our meeting, and the energy was palpable. In my enthusiasm, I invited anyone who was sick to come forward for prayer, expecting a few people. To my surprise, around five hundred lined up, each hoping for healing.

I remember the exhaustion of praying for each person, but what struck me most was that nothing seemed to happen. Despite our fervent prayers, no one appeared to receive any healing. Some people even circled back to the end of the line, waiting for another chance. One man came forward, complaining of pain in his legs. I thought, somewhat frustrated, *Do you think you have sore legs? I've been standing here forever.*

The longer we prayed, the more frustrated I became. I knew Jesus healed—I had witnessed it countless times—but it felt like He chose not to heal anyone in La Cruz that day.

Yet another person approached, and I asked, "What would you like prayer for?"

"I can't hear in my left ear; please pray," he replied.

So, I prayed, even laying my hands on his ear. "Can you hear me now?" I asked, hoping for a breakthrough.

He shook his finger, indicating "no" in that familiar Mexican way.

Something snapped inside me. Without thinking, I blurted out, "Stupid ear, open up!" Fortunately, I said it in English so he wouldn't be offended.

Suddenly, the man shouted, "What? I can hear! I can hear!" He began jumping around, excitedly telling everyone that his hearing had been restored.

Encouraged, I called the next person forward. "I have no sense of smell," he said when I asked what he needed prayer for.

I looked around and asked if anyone had perfume. After someone handed me a bottle, I poured a generous amount onto my wrist. "Here, can you smell this?" I asked, holding my wrist to his nose.

"No, nothing," he replied.

"All right, let's pray." I prayed in Spanish, asking the Lord to heal his sense of smell. Then, I held my wrist to his nose again.

"No, nothing," he repeated.

By now, all my encouragement from the previous healing was fading fast, and frustration started to take over. Once again, in English, I muttered, "Stupid nose, open up."

When I put my wrist up to his nose this time, his eyes widened in astonishment. "I can smell! I can smell!" he shouted. Overjoyed, he began telling everyone around him what the Lord had done.

That moment seemed to break something open, and before we knew it, hundreds of people were healed and saved that first night in La Cruz. At the end of the service, a man approached us and offered to let us use his building in the center of town to start the church. What took us five years to start in the first town, God accomplished in just one night in La Cruz.

Over time, we planted five churches north of Mazatlán, including San Ignacio, and the churches remain. I learned many valuable lessons along the way. Above all, I understood the truth in Psalm 127:1:

> *Unless the* Lord *builds the house,*
> *They labor in vain who build it;*
> *Unless the* Lord *guards the city,*
> *The watchman stays awake in vain."*

Those healings had nothing to do with me—I had practically given up, as my frustrated language made evident. In those moments of weakness, God's strength was the clearest. I know now that I cannot walk on water in my strength—it must always be the Lord who sustains me. He builds the house. He opens ears and noses and eyes and hearts. And when He begins something, He will see it through to completion.

The Right Place at the Right Time

As the Lord leads us and we keep our eyes on Him, we end up in amazing places and have divine appointments.

One day, I said, "We should do baptisms in the river instead of the ocean." La Cruz is right by the sea, and we had always enjoyed baptizing people in the waves, but I wanted to try something new this time. So, we loaded everyone into my pickup truck and headed to the river.

To get there, we had to cross a high bridge I'd never been on before. While driving, we noticed a girl sitting on the railing, talking to a guy on a motorcycle. One of the team members shouted, "I think she is thinking of jumping." Right as he said that, everyone gasped, and she jumped.

"She did it," he said in shock. Fortunately, the guy on the motorcycle caught her by the ankle, leaving her hanging thirty feet above the road. We rushed over to help him pull her up.

She was hysterical as we sat her on the curb, trying to calm her down. "I want to die," she kept repeating.

I noticed she had a hospital band on her wrist. "Settle down. We'll take you to the hospital," I reassured her.

We got everyone back into the truck, but as we pulled away, she continued screaming and thrashing about.

People might think we're kidnapping her, I thought, so I quickly stopped the truck and turned to the girl. "If you don't calm down, we'll take you to the police instead," I warned her.

That seemed to work—she settled down. Since she did not want to go to the police or the hospital, we took her to the house where we held services.

The girls took her inside the house while I got to work setting up for our church service and preparing for worship. After a couple of hours, people began arriving for church. I noticed the girls who had been with the distraught girl were now seated, but I didn't see the girl from the bridge.

"What happened to her?" I asked them. "Where is she?"

"She's right here," they said, presenting what seemed like a completely different girl. "She gave her life to Jesus, and He saved her and healed her broken heart."

> I had never witnessed such an instant and complete transformation before.

I had never witnessed such an instant and complete transformation before. She was a new creation, safe and in her right mind. She was so changed that I didn't even recognize her.

We had never been on that bridge before, yet the Lord led us to cross it at the exact moment when she needed help. I marvel at how the Lord directs our steps and uses His people to seek and save the lost. Our job is to focus on Him and follow His lead; His job is to ensure we are in the right place at the right time.

The Dangers We See— And the Dangers We Don't

Let me share one last story to illustrate how God watches out for us when we stay focused on Him, even when we are unaware of the dangers around us.

We had brought a pastor from the city named Gilberto to La Cruz. He was a wonderful person with many admirable traits but came with city customs that didn't quite fit in the pueblo. In the city, it's common for people to greet women with an air kiss on the cheek, but that is not the case in the pueblos. When Gilberto greeted the women in La Cruz the same way, he unknowingly offended their husbands.

"That stupid pastor you sent is hitting on our women. What will you do about it?" one man asked me.

I didn't realize it at the time, but this man was the primary drug lord in the town. I explained to him that this kind of friendly, cheek-to-cheek kiss was a common custom in the city and that Gilberto had no intention of taking their wives.

After that, things seemed to calm down, and I told Gilberto to stop kissing the ladies to avoid further misunderstanding.

The following week, Dave—another pastor from Mazatlán—and Gilberto went to La Cruz for services. Afterward, they decided to take the toll road to get home faster, even though the free highway, which takes about thirty minutes longer, was an option.

Two days later, I returned to town and visited the man who had been offended by Gilberto. "Where did your guys go after the service?" he asked me. I told him they had taken the toll road home.

"You're lucky," he said coldly. "My boys and I were waiting for them by the entrance to the free road." Then he showed me his machine guns. "You better never bring that guy back to town," he warned.

They had unknowingly escaped with their lives. The man I was dealing with was a severe threat, and we did not know it at the time.

How many threats and traps has the Lord delivered us from while we walk on water? When we keep our eyes on the Lord, He leads, protects, provides, and saves us from dangers—both the ones we see and the ones we do not.

CHAPTER 8

WE NEVER LOOK BACK, AND WE DON'T LOOK DOWN

"Remember Lot's wife."

Luke 17:32

Lot's wife looked back while fleeing Sodom, despite the Lord's warning: "Escape for your life! Do not look behind you, nor stay anywhere in the plain" (Genesis 19:17). It's surprising how stubbornly Lot's family clung to the past. Even though their surroundings were deeply corrupt, they were attached to their place. Despite their excuses and delays, they eventually fled. But Lot's wife looked back and was turned into a pillar of salt—a monument to teach us not to dwell on the past. We must move forward, not back to the "glory days." We might recall the revival of the Jesus Movement, the holy laughter of 1994, or even our first church experiences. We remember, but we don't want to return there. The best is yet to come.

When Mary Jo and I married in 1984, we committed, "Till death do us part." There is no other option: I'm blessed with her for the rest of our lives, and she's stuck with me. We joke together all the time, but never about divorce. We don't look back or seek other options. We love the inheritance the Lord has given us, and our time together gets better and more joyful each year. There are countless blessings in never looking back.

Bye, Bye Mazatlán

By 1998, the signs were clear: our time in Mazatlán had ended. Mary Jo and I sat in the empty church building praying. "We will pray until the Lord shows us what to do," I said, and Mary Jo agreed.

When we set out to plant churches in Mexico, we partnered with two missionary couples to establish a mother church in the city. One couple from the U.S. had moved to Mazatlán a few years before us, and by the time we arrived, the church had grown to about seventy people.

At first, working together felt natural—we complemented each other well, and the church flourished. Growth came quickly, and the ministry thrived. But as the years passed, something shifted. Instead of complementing one another, we found ourselves competing. What had once been a strong partnership became a struggle for direction and influence.

After seven years, tensions with the first couple had become unavoidable. Conflict crept in, making it clear that something had to change. We knew we couldn't rely on our wisdom—we needed to seek God's guidance in prayer to understand what He was calling us to do next.

"I have a vision of us stuck in the mud," Mary Jo said after a few minutes of prayer. Her vision hit like a ton of bricks.

I did not want to waste my time stuck in the mud, and I knew a little about what to do if I was stuck. You don't just spin your wheels if you're stuck in the mud. You need to get radical.

So we invited the other pastors to our house to discuss it. Mary Jo and I were determined to find a solution to our problem.

We sat in our living room, which overlooked the jungle out back, and awkwardly faced the other couple we had worked with for years. "What do you think we should do?" I asked.

The wife looked at me and answered, "We think you should leave."

Her words were a bucket of cold water, but they confirmed the problem we faced. They did not want to keep working with us, and after seven years of helping the church grow and planting five churches north of the city, they wanted us out.

> When a door slams in your face, keeping your eyes on Jesus isn't easy.

When a door slams in your face, keeping your eyes on Jesus isn't easy. I can evaluate how we reached that point in our relationship, but now I know it was another invitation from Jesus to step out and see miracles.

Once again, we were in uncharted waters. People pleaded with us to stay and start another church. "I will never cause a church split," I told Mary Jo.

The transition was very tough for our family. We were rooted deep in Mazatlán, and our friends could not understand why we would abandon them. My son, who was just ten years old, was devastated to lose his friends. "I'll be your friend," I told him, but it was little comfort.

We were very tempted to look back at the past or look down at the waves beneath us. But we fixed our eyes on Jesus, and the joy set before us. We knew we had to go, but we needed to know where. It was like Abraham all over again. "Go out, and I will show you," the Lord said.

We gathered two couples and a single woman, and a little over a month later, we moved south to Tepic, Nayarit. Since the team members were from the beach and loved to surf, we thought our ultimate destination was Puerto Vallarta, but we moved to Tepic, a city about halfway between Mazatlán and Puerto Vallarta, to spy out the land from a closer place.

My friend Bruce ran the Youth With A Mission base in Tepic, and during our transition, he graciously offered us a place to stay in the house he used as a base. One of the couples remained in Mazatlán for six months because the wife was pregnant, and the others moved with us. We had one room, and the other couple took the other available spot. We pushed two bunk beds together, and the kids slept on the top while Mary Jo and I took the bottom.

Paulo, one of the people who came with us, helped me knock on doors in Puerto Vallarta. We made several three-and-a-half-hour trips to Puerto Vallarta and even spent a week looking for an open door, but nothing opened up for us. We returned to Tepic defeated. I knew the Lord was calling us to start a church but did not know where to do it.

Upon our return from Puerto Vallarta, Bruce asked, "Why don't you plant a church here in Tepic?"

It hit me. Why not Tepic? It became clear, like I was a blind man seeing for the first time. After a bit more prayer and counsel, we decided to plant ourselves in Tepic. We often say the will of God is perfect in retrospect, and it is true. The Lord prepared us for years for this time and place.

Growing Pains

We rented an old auto shop on the back side of a bad neighborhood and started our first church service in July of 1998. We prayed that people would come or even be able to find us. The only bathroom was behind the main building, on the far end of a junkyard. People had to walk through the dark and around the garbage every time they needed to use the bathroom. The metal roof was low and very loud in the rain. It was hard even to reach the building because every road around the shop had been dug up, forcing us to walk around piles of dirt and deep ditches. When it wasn't raining, we moved all the equipment to a nearby park and held our services there, preferring the open air to that place.

I remember one evening event in particular. We had a guest speaker, and as he began to preach, he said, "I am speaking today on—" The bus out front revved its motor so loud it drowned out his voice.

He started over. "Once again, I am going to share about—" The band next door started blaring music.

He tried one last time. "I am speaking on—" The rain started drumming on the roof.

"I give up!" the speaker yelled at me over the racket. So we had to shut down that night.

The shop owner approached me asking for more rent. Since we rarely used the building, I was not very open to the idea. "If you want more rent, we will move," I told him. Instead of negotiating or offering to help fix stuff, he complained and talked about his problems. We were in the worst possible building and had to get out.

Soon after, a friend told me a nearby church was leaving their building. I asked where and proceeded to spy on them as they emptied the building. As soon as possible, I arranged a meeting with the owner. He accepted a meeting but was suspicious of me.

"Can you pay the rent?" he asked suspiciously, as the other church always struggled to pay the rent.

I assured him we would pay, and with some difficulty, we made a deal.

"This place is perfect," I said, looking over the second-floor building that would hold close to one hundred people. It was right on the main road, with a view of the fire station in front. I knew we had found a perfect location.

After overcoming his suspicion, Daniel, the building owner, became a faithful church member and a great friend to me. "I'm going to the crazy party church," he would say as he left for church each week.

> That is walking on water—you step out and expect God to carry you.

The church grew quickly, and soon we needed more room.

"I can rent you the bottom floor," Daniel said.

He offered a great price, but it was still more than double what we paid in rent. Jesus always asks us to take steps of faith, and the rent was a significant step. That is walking on water—you step out and expect God to carry you. We agreed to the deal. With room for two hundred and fifty, the church grew even quicker, and the giving increased, allowing us never to miss the rent payment.

Repair the Ruins

God was clearly not looking back or down—He was looking onward and upward, and it was our job to keep up. For me, that often meant changing the way I thought about certain things. For example, I didn't want to cause division or problems with other churches, so I was hesitant to receive anyone from another church.

"I want to attend your church, but I go to another church in town," a man named Joshua pleaded with me.

"You need to stay in your church. I did not come here to take people from other churches," I answered.

He returned two or three times, asking to come to our church. Then, while praying, I read a verse:

> *And they shall rebuild the old ruins,*
> *They shall raise up the former desolations,*
> *And they shall repair the ruined cities,*
> *The desolations of many generations.*
> *(Isaiah 61:4)*

Before we arrived in Tepic, some existing pastors and churches had suffered from division and immorality, leaving people in ruins. "You need to repair the ruins," the Lord told me.

So, the next time I saw Joshua, I told him he was welcome to attend. The following Sunday, over twenty people came with him. He has an extensive family. Our church started just in time to be a refuge for many needy people. I saw the perfect timing of the Lord as we followed Him on the water.

They Stole the Truck

"Never look back and don't look down" is easy to say, but it will be tested. When bad things happen, that's when the choice to keep moving onward and upward is most important.

As we began the church in Tepic, we received some funds for new sound equipment. Excited, our family set out on a shopping trip to Guadalajara with another couple. We started at the sound equipment store, where we found great speakers and gear, and then spent the afternoon visiting other shops. In the afternoon, we stopped at Costco, loaded two carts with supplies, and headed to the truck for home. But as we approached the parking lot, my heart sank—my truck was gone.

"I can't believe it. Someone stole my truck," I said in disbelief as we frantically searched the area.

Panic set in as I realized the speakers and equipment were still in the truck, along with our passports and $400 in cash in the glove box. *I'm ruined*, I thought.

I quickly ran to call the police. "What's the license plate number?" the officer asked.

I froze—I didn't know, so I had to call home to ask someone to dig through my paperwork. As I was spiraling, my daughter Rebecca tugged at my hand, asking me to go to the bathroom. In the middle of all the chaos, I took her hand and walked to a nearby restaurant.

That's when I heard a whisper in my mind: "What do you have in your hand?"

I looked down at my beautiful little girl. And suddenly, it hit me—I hadn't lost what mattered most. I still had Rebecca.

"Be at peace," I felt God telling me.

That moment of encouragement carried me through the challenging season ahead. I was still making monthly payments on the truck, and my tourist insurance took an entire year to come through. In the meantime, I had to keep up with the payments on a vehicle I did not have and borrow money to buy a small car, which meant even more debt. When the insurance finally paid out, I was in deep financial trouble and had no idea how I would get out.

But that gentle reminder kept me grounded. I hadn't lost the most important things in life, and somehow, I knew I would find a way forward.

House Fires and Car Wrecks

"The house burned down last night, but everyone is safe," my sister told me over the phone. Thankfully, my mother and sister had good insurance, so they moved into trailers on the property while cleaning up and preparing to rebuild. However, the builders didn't meet my mother's expectations and ignored her input.

One day, she had enough. "Son, I hate what they're doing with the house. I want you to take over," my mom said.

"You've got to be kidding me," I replied, but I knew she was serious.

Thus began a series of ten flights from Mexico to Seattle, each trip bringing me closer to finishing the reconstruction.

On the tenth and final flight, the whole family came along. "I'm so excited," I told Mary Jo as we rented a small car for the two-hour drive to my mother's house. "With this trip, I'll finally earn enough to pay off all our debts."

We spent a few days at my mom's, finishing the remaining tasks. With everything completed and a check in hand, we loaded the family into the car and headed back to the city. It was a typical rainy day in Western Washington, and I was eager to reach the hotel where we'd stay before flying out for a speaking engagement the following day.

But as we sped along the wet road, I took a hairpin turn too fast. The brakes locked, and suddenly, the car veered off the cliff, crashing into two trees that miraculously stopped our fall. The airbags deployed, filling the car with smoke, and for a terrifying moment, we wondered if the vehicle was on fire. Mary Jo's door was pinned against one of the trees, and she could only escape by crawling into the back seat.

I still remember the scene. The whole Hansen family was lying on the side of the little country road. I was bleeding from my head, and everyone was sore and shocked. I lay on the road awaiting the ambulance and suffering from self-incrimination.

"I am the worst father, driver, and husband; I'm such an idiot, I started to say. "I was getting out of debt, but now I am even worse than before."

Knowing I should not say such a thing, Mary Jo told me to shut my mouth.

She is right, I thought, and I zipped my lips shut. However, although I silenced my words, I didn't silence my thoughts. I started adding up the costs, wondering if the rental car insurance I carried on my credit card would pay for this mess.

Then the police showed up, and the officer told my sister, who had come as soon as she heard we crashed, that he was issuing me a ticket for reckless driving. My sister was persuasive and informed the officer that we were missionaries who had come to help, so he relented.

Costs piled up in my mind as the ambulance arrived. Once at the hospital, the doctor treated my head wound, carefully stapling it closed. How much will this cost? I wondered but kept silent. Even the bandage they brought for Rebecca felt like a financial strain. *Just shut your mouth and trust God,* I reminded myself. Despite my anxiety, I began to praise Him—grateful that we were alive and still in His hands.

By morning, I was sore but encouraged. I had a flight to Phoenix to preach and considered canceling. But a friend's words echoed in my mind: "You can't cancel and let the devil win." So, I pushed through my worry step by step, trusting God as I walked on water.

After filing an insurance claim for the totaled rental car, I explained how the brakes had locked up, causing the vehicle to skid on the rain-soaked road. Their response? "We do not cover defects to the vehicle or road hazards."

Frustrated, I thought, *Then what do you cover?* I sent them the police report, which described my driving as reckless—a conclusion I disagreed with but included nonetheless. To my surprise, they accepted the claim and covered the costs.

Miraculously, the accident didn't cost me a dime or add to my debts. I remained debt-free, free to continue dancing on the water, and stronger for overcoming my worry and self-doubt.

There Is a Building

One of the greatest examples of dancing on the water and never looking back has been the miraculous purchase of our building. I share some of this story in my book *Who Will Stay?*, but I'm including more details here because the journey was difficult.

I was at a church in Washington State. A visiting speaker was ministering to the children, and a couple hundred kids were in a line before the stage. I stood in the front row with my eyes closed, dressed in a suit and tie because we still had to wear those awful things back then.

Suddenly, someone grabbed me by the tie and pulled me forward with the kids. It was the visiting speaker. "There's a building waiting for you. When you get home, you need to find it," he told me.

At the time, he had never met me and did not know who I was. Later, I met him and even had pastor Tim Bagwell visit me in Mexico. I have become great friends with his son, Aaron Bagwell, who runs a wonderful ministry to children worldwide called Expect Hope.

Upon returning to Mexico, I gathered our staff and said, "A building is waiting for us. We need to find it."

Soon, one of the pastors told me, "The building called La Fuente is for sale."

I knew La Fuente since we rented it for a Christmas program. It was in a great location, and it was a huge building compared to where we met, so I figured it was way out of our reach financially.

"The building costs two million pesos," the real estate agent told us. At the time, that was $200,000. I couldn't believe it, so I asked to meet with the owner.

I offered fifteen thousand dollars in down payment and the rest in a year. It was a very low offer but not unheard of in Mexico. I cannot write the numerous cuss words the owner used, but he wanted me to know that he did not like gringos who offered such a bad deal, then he stormed out of the office. *Oops, I think I blew that*, I told myself.

I called a friend of mine who had made numerous deals and asked for his advice. "You need to sweeten the deal," he said. Then I learned that the owner had taken a loan on the building and was paying one thousand six hundred dollars a month.

In our next meeting, I told him, "We will give you thirty thousand down and two thousand a month, and we'll pay off the balance in one year."

He said, "Yes."

I was stunned. I did not have the money I offered him. "Could you give me a couple weeks to get the thirty thousand?" I asked.

He agreed, and I was on the water again. This time, it was the biggest deal of my life. We explained the need to the church, and our two-hundred-member church gave $20,000 in one offering, which allowed us to make the down payment. We saw many miracles after that, and within a year, we had paid one hundred thousand dollars toward the purchase.

That's awesome—but if you're doing the math, we were still a hundred thousand short, and our time was up. Once again, I found myself thinking, *It's never easy, is it?*

We discussed the situation while visiting my friend, pastor Ron Smedley, in his church in Glendale, California. As more people moved into the area around Ron's church, it had become an Armenian neighborhood, and Ron's small congregation was not equipped to reach them. In addition, there was no parking for the people.

> We were still a hundred thousand short, and our time was up.

"You don't serve this place anymore, and it doesn't serve you. You should sell it and find a new location, and when you do, lend me the money to pay off La Fuente," I jokingly told Ron as we visited. Soon, I returned home, and I even forgot our conversation.

Then Ron called. "I know you were joking when you told me to sell, but we decided you were right. When we sell, we want to loan you the funds to pay off your building."

I was ecstatic. I had a way to save the deal. I explained the situation to the owner and asked him to give us six months more. He graciously agreed and even lowered our monthly payment, so it looked like I had avoided a bullet. He could have pulled the deal if he had wanted to, and we would have had difficulty getting our money back.

I was preaching for a friend at a church in Arizona when I received a call from Ron. "Dwight, our building sold, and we have a new location, but my board is trying to back out of loaning you the money. You must get to LA to see if you can salvage the deal."

My heart sank. I had made promises, and like the wind hitting Peter's faith, I could feel myself sinking. The next day, I rushed to LA to attend their board meeting.

"Because you are my friend, I have to stay neutral," Ron said.

One board member, a businessman, constantly criticized the loan, while another was always positive. In this meeting, they switched roles. The positive member squirmed and sweated as he said he thought they should not loan me the money. "I feel like we may need it in the future, and I am afraid of what might happen in this economy," he said.

The members began to argue and negotiate, and I felt the deal falling apart. Ron stayed quiet as they argued back and forth.

Then, when things couldn't get more intense, the very member who had initially supported the deal—but had now turned against it—suddenly bolted to the bathroom and threw up. The spiritual oppression in the room was almost tangible. Darkness pressed in, and a heavy weight settled over the conversation.

Suddenly, the businessman, who had always been negative, shouted, "This is ridiculous! We promised to loan Dwight the money and must keep our word. Now I'm late for another meeting, so let's finish this."

Once he spoke, it felt like demons fled the room. With the air cleared, the board voted to loan us the money we needed to buy La Fuente.

When we receive supernatural provisions, we often remain unaware of the intricate workings behind the scenes. The Lord frequently uses willing individuals to meet our needs, orchestrating circumstances by aligning human wills. However, this alignment can sometimes be a struggle, as stepping into the unknown requires faith and courage.

Many miracles hinge on others being willing to step out onto the water with us, partnering in faith and action. Yet, when someone lends a hand, it doesn't negate the Lord's involvement or diminish the miraculous nature of the provision. Instead, it highlights that we are co-laborers with Christ and others.

CHAPTER 9

STINKING THINKING LEADS TO SINKING

Set your mind on things above, not on things on the earth.

Colossians 3:2

Moses was very bold. After convincing God not to abandon His people, he asked for more. "Please, show me Your glory" (Exodus 33:18). The Lord agreed and told Moses that He would put him in the cleft of the rock and cover him with His hand while He passed by.

This story illustrates how we walk on water. Just as Moses hid in the rock, we are hidden in Christ. When we are "in Christ," we can defy the natural law of gravity.

Years ago, in a small traditional church, my friend Glen and I sang along to the old hymn, "He Hideth My Soul." The chorus is terrific.

> *He hideth my soul in the cleft of the rock*
> *That shadows a dry, thirsty land.*

> He hideth my life in the depths of His love
> And covers me there with His hand.³

While I was singing, I kicked off my shoes for some reason. Then, as we sang the verses, Glen hid one of my shoes. I was looking for it when the chorus started: "He hideth my soul in the cleft of the rock." Glen leaned over and said, "I've hidden thy sole in the cleft of the pew."

The incident was funny, but the song's lyrics—and the truth behind it—have stayed with me. I am hidden in Christ. My life is safe in His love. That truth has sustained me in many difficult moments.

Jesus told us to abide in Him, and He said that apart from Him, we cannot do anything. We must abide in Christ by faith every day. I am in Christ. He is my cleft in the Rock. He is my righteousness, sanctification, and redemption. My continued faith in Christ upholds me and allows me to do the miraculous.

The evil one constantly sows unbelief and doubt and tries to draw our attention to the dangers around us. I call these tactics devil bombs. Constant explosions of fear and doubt cause us to get our eyes off Jesus and onto the wind. He wants us to look down or look back, anything but look to Jesus. But when we abide in God's word, we can dance on the water.

---

3 Fanny J. Crosby, "He Hideth My Soul," *The Finest of the Wheat* (Chicago: R. R. McCabe, 1890).

We have learned to capture our rebellious thoughts and focus our minds on Christ. We have learned to keep putting one foot in front of the other. We know that the One who began this walk will finish it. He invited us to follow and always gives us the grace to take another step.

Devil Been Talkin'

In 2011, I fell from a balcony that we were tearing down. I broke my ankle and tore all the ligaments that held it together. The doctor put it back together with seven screws and a titanium plate, but it was ten weeks until I could start to use it again. I still remember preaching in a wheelchair and being mocked by children as I slowly drove around Walmart in a cart.

The inactivity was very hard for me. I spent too much time thinking about depressing things such as: *You are a loser. Your recklessness caused this. You are not getting anything done.*

As a result of the depression and inactivity, I gained about fifty pounds. Thoughts came to me without realizing what was happening: *You should be prepared to die. You could go anytime, so you should think about it. It looks like you are done. You have had a good life; now it is time for others to take over.* At the time, all the thoughts seemed practical and logical.

Mary Jo was getting concerned, so I took a step and applied for health insurance. The results of my physical came back, and they appeared great. I had low cholesterol, and the blood work looked favorable to us. We were surprised to hear that they rejected me.

"Why? Everything looks fine," I asked. I was informed the test results showed way too high of numbers for my liver. I had fatty liver.

On hearing the report, Mary Jo told me I needed to change my eating habits.

"If I can't eat, why even live?" I grumbled.

But she was right, and with her help, I changed my diet. She prepared meals that were much better than the junk food I was used to eating.

Then, she introduced me to Walking at Home videos, and I began exercising. When I started, my body screamed, "You can't do this. You are too stiff and old. Don't think that you can start exercising now."

I needed to change my thinking. I was accepting too many lies and excuses. At the time, we often listened to a group called *Needtobreathe*, and one of their songs was titled "Devil's Been Talkin'." That summed up my problem. I was listening to the wrong voice.

Stinking thinking leads to sinking. We love to make excuses for our weaknesses, failures, and sins, but we won't have excuses in heaven. There is a Mexican proverb I like: "When they invented excuses, they did away with fools." This implies that once people learn how to make excuses, they can cover up their foolishness. In other words, you no longer appear foolish if you have a good excuse. People often make excuses instead of accepting responsibility for their actions.

No one needs a depressed father or leader. I needed to get back up and fight. I needed to stop being a victim and quit making excuses. I quit eating certain foods and started to exercise. I had another physical, and after losing fifty pounds, my liver results came back at normal levels, and I was able to get insurance. The problem was not just physical. I had to change my thinking. I had to get my eyes off myself and back on Jesus.

> I had to change my thinking. I had to get my eyes off myself and back on Jesus.

For years, we have taught people about the battle of the mind. Evil thoughts lead to evil deeds. Adam and Eve chatted with the serpent, and his deception led to the fall of man. We cannot afford to sit around chatting with the devil. But his lies are subtle, and often, we think they are simply our thoughts.

Learning to identify when thoughts are not our own and to capture and cast them out is a big part of maturing. "But solid food belongs to those who are of full age, that is, those who by reason of use have their senses exercised to discern both good and evil" (Hebrews 5:14). Discernment comes through practice, and so does walking on water.

Armchair Quarterbacks

Reading the story of Peter walking on the water always raises questions: "Why did only Peter ask to walk on the water?" "What were the other disciples doing?" "What would have happened if everyone asked to do it and got out to walk with Peter?" "Were they impressed by what Peter did, or did they mock him when he sank?" No matter what happened, Peter did it, and they stayed in the boat. They remained in a safe place and watched the drama like armchair quarterbacks.

Many stay in the boat and criticize how well you are walking. They love to compare you to great water walkers they have watched before. They quickly offer a tip or rebuke, but they are still in the boat. It is easy to criticize and analyze why others fail, but you have nothing to say if you are still in the boat.

When you are the one on the water, one sure way to stop dancing and start sinking is to worry about what others think of you. "You are not called to lead. It is not your gift. You have an anger issue; you are too loud, too much of a clown. You are too charismatic; you are not charismatic enough. You are not anointed. You don't know what you are doing." Those are just a few things they shouted at me from the boat.

I enjoy clowning around and playing while we work hard. I have often looked at others who are so solemn and who seem more profound and spiritual than I am. I have tried to be like them several times but failed. Then, one day, I thought, *I like jokes. I enjoy having fun with my friends in ministry.* That is when I embraced who God made me to be. I became comfortable in my skin. I also got a backbone and stopped listening to the whispers of the serpent.

We need right thinking about ourselves—being comfortable in our own skin and accountable to God, not to the shifting opinions, worries, or critiques of others. At the same time, we need right thinking about others. That means refusing to let slander, accusation, or suspicion take root in our hearts.

Accusation and suspicion are potent tools in the devil's toolkit. He thrives on sowing discord among brothers and sisters because the moment we fix our eyes on each other with judgment or doubt, we take our eyes off Jesus—and begin to sink.

Remember: he is the accuser of the brethren. Suspicion is not a gift of the Spirit. The devil may be whispering lies about your brother, and if you believe them, you're walking straight into his trap.

The accusers (and the loudest critics) often end up sinking beneath the waves. I see the fruit of their pride, bitterness, and hatred as I grow older. It's tragic—so much destruction begins with a single offense.

The Greek word for "offense" is the root of our English word scandal. Originally, it described a trap, snare, or stumbling block: something designed to make someone fall or lose their way.

In the book *The Bait of Satan*, John Bevere explains that offenses are bait. The world and the enemy use offenses to "hook" us, pulling us into the dark waters of bitterness and division.

> The true successes are those who get out on the field, take risks and give it their all.

But the heart of the gospel is love—love for God and love for people. And one of the quickest ways to destroy that love is through offense.

Do you remember when Jesus allowed a woman to pour expensive oil over his head? The disciples were indignant and outraged that some woman would do that. But above all, it was a waste of money. It is incredible how righteous and offended we can get over cash. Although indignant, eleven disciples got over it once Jesus explained that she anointed him for burial. However, one used the offense as a motive to betray Jesus. Satan entered Judas Iscariot through an offense.

"I am not offended; I am hurt," a pastor told me years ago. I explained that it was the same thing.

Amazingly, we can use religious words to cloak our wounds and offenses. He remained offended even after I asked him to forgive me for things I never did. His offense pulled him further away, like a hook in a fish's mouth. He left offended after that, and he is still bitter today.

Jesus promised us that "offenses must come" (Matthew 18:7). We never try to offend people, but sometimes it is unavoidable. Walking on the water means we keep following Jesus even if it offends someone or they criticize our actions. Armchair quarterbacks don't win games. The true successes are those who get out on the field, take risks and give it their all.

The Power of Teamwork

"I will go, but I don't want to go alone," I told the Lord when I knew He was leading us to start a church in Tepic.

So, in 1998, we gathered a small team. Each team member pulled their weight, the Lord blessed our unity, and things started to grow quickly. A pastor joined us, and his wife did an incredible job with the children while he focused on pastoral care and teaching. Within a year, we grew to over 250 in Sunday attendance. A year and a half later, we purchased our building on the main avenue in town, and attendance skyrocketed to over 600. It was one of the clearest examples of the power of teamwork that I have experienced.

Recognizing the value of teamwork is a key element of right thinking. The dictionary defines synergy as "the combined power of a group of things when they are working together that is greater than the total power achieved by each working separately."4 For example, I've read that two horses working together can pull more than twice what one can pull alone.

The power of teamwork is irrefutable. A football team can win the Super Bowl if it practices and prepares. A band that collaborates can compose the best music. Soldiers who train together and coordinate their movements can win wars.

I imagine that Peter and all the disciples would have walked to Jesus on the water and never sunk if they had walked as a team. I cannot be sure, but I know the power of teamwork. Jesus had personally called each person in the boat, and all of them had left their old lives behind to follow Jesus—yet they were content to let Peter do the heavy lifting of faith. Like the disciples in the boat, many people are content to let others walk in faith. They say, "Here am I—send him."

People often fall into hero worship because of this preference to watch others take risks and do the work. As humans, we have an innate desire for

---

4 "Synergy," Cambridge University Press & Assessment, https://dictionary.cambridge.org/dictionary/english/synergy#google_vignette.

a king. We are not content with the Lord's authority; we want to give another person the credit and let them take on the responsibility that should be ours. Like Israel, we want a king. "And the Lord said to Samuel, 'Heed the voice of the people in all that they say to you; for they have not rejected you, but they have rejected Me, that I should not reign over them'" (1 Samuel 8:7). The problem is, we will never dance on the water if we don't get out of the boat—together with the team—and do our part to move forward.

Other people want to be heroes, leading them to abandon teamwork and do things on their own. They see the person in charge and think, "I can do that. It's my time. I need to build something on my own. I want to leave a legacy. I don't want to work for another person's vision. This place will fall apart without me." These are all sayings we hear when someone no longer wants to be on the team. They swallow the lie that they can do better on their own. But without the team, they often sink quicker than Peter.

In general, they would do much better if they continued to work on a team. Even if the Lord moves them to another team, they should still be part of a team, not out on their own, attempting to be the hero and king. That's not how God designed humans to function best. "Two are better than one, because they have a good reward for their labor" (Ecclesiastes 4:9).

Of course, when a key team member leaves, it's not easy. "True pastors cry a little even when the devil leaves," I told my pastor friend Mike, who told me about some leaders who left the church he pastors in Texas. If you are a pastor, you should love the flock that the Lord has entrusted to you. However, we all deal with feelings of personal rejection and sadness when people leave.

Some changes are necessary, and God can use the adjustments for good. As one pastor said, "The church is a body, and every healthy body needs a bowel movement occasionally."

When people want to leave, I have learned to let them go graciously. I am not the Holy Spirit and don't control where He calls people. My mentality is, "If you can recruit them, you can have them." We plant and water, but God grows the church. As leaders, part of our job is sending workers into the harvest, which may require change and separation. It's funny—we pray and train young leaders to do what we do, and then we are surprised when they want to do what we do.

Teamwork is powerful, but not all teams are good teams. A few hundred years after the flood, people came together to build the Tower of Babel. Everyone spoke the same language, and they decided to build a tower. They wanted to build a tower to the heavens and make a name for themselves so they would not be scattered worldwide. Interestingly, the tower was in the same area as Babylon in modern-day southern Iraq. Though full of pride and rebellion, the people accomplished a lot through teamwork. So much so that God came down, saw the tower, and confirmed the power of teamwork.

> *"And the LORD said, "Indeed the people are one and they all have one language, and this is what they begin to do; now nothing that they propose to do will be withheld from them" (Genesis 11:6).*

In this case, God confused and scattered them because they were an evil, rebellious team without the Lord at the top. Teams can become selfish and prideful, and the Lord often breaks up teams that become self-seeking and envious. When a team falls apart, don't give up on teamwork. Instead, seek a healthier team that aligns with your values and vision rather than abandoning the concept altogether.

> Nothing kills teamwork faster than evil thoughts.

I don't know what you are thinking about those who walk with you on the water, but nothing kills teamwork faster than evil thoughts. "For where envy and self-seeking exist, confusion and every evil thing are there" (James 3:16). As soon as we stop thinking right about God, others, and ourselves, we sink like a stone.

Terror Makes for Stinking Thinking

Fear and worry have a way of poisoning our minds and controlling our actions. If we are going to dance on the water, we must capture these negative thoughts and stop our stinking thinking.

In years past, Tepic was always known as one of the most peaceful cities in Mexico. All that changed in 2008. The cartels fought a turf war in Tepic. We went from the safest city in Mexico to the fifth most violent city in the world. Along with the drug war, many kidnappers, con artists, and other criminals converged on Tepic.

Many people made substantial life decisions in reaction to the violence and fear that swept through our region. Their eyes were turned from Jesus to the wind and waves, and many wavered in their faith.

But not everyone responded that way. One woman stands out in my mind. Her name is Krisna, and she is a small woman with a big heart. Krisna was on a small bus full of people as it passed a supermarket. Gunshots rang out as her bus pulled up to the stop. The people fighting even had hand grenades.

"Hit the deck," someone yelled, and everyone got down.

Except for Krisna. She stood in front of the bus. "Do not fear! The Lord is with us. You need to make sure you are right with the Lord," she shouted above the noise.

The violence hit especially close to home one day when my son wanted me to take him to see a movie at the mall. I don't remember what we watched, but as we left the theater, we noticed the lobby was locked down and we could not leave.

"What's going on?" we asked the attendant.

"There has been a shooting in the parking lot," she replied, "but we will open soon."

They let us go shortly after that, and we walked through the mall to get to our car. Suddenly, a wave of people came running right at us. Later, we learned that the suspect had shot an officer in the National Guard and then fled into the mall. We dove into a women's clothing store to hide. The blouses and bras did not appear to be the best protection from bullets, so we moved to a closet in the back of the store. The closet was not much safer.

Suddenly, my phone rang. It was my friend Tony. "Hey, pray for me," he said. "There has been a shooting at the mall, and we are hiding in a closet on the second floor."

"That makes two of us," I replied. "I'm right beneath you on the first floor."

Soon, they caught the shooter, and we got the all-clear.

Another dramatic incident happened on the Saturday before a big event at the church. Four gang members decided to try to break some people out of the state prison a few blocks from our main church building in Tepic. As they started shooting, a whole group of federal police pulled up to the prison, and they quickly took action against the attackers.

The four men fled up the boulevard, where they crashed into a telephone pole in front of our church, with fierce, angry police on their tail. They shot one suspect right there. Two other suspects fled toward our church's back door right as Ame, a girl on staff, stepped inside. They pushed into the church, where several young people were preparing for our event. As our students hid in the back, the suspects ran up the stairs to an apartment where some of our guys lived. Fortunately, they were not there at the time. The young people heard the shots ring out as the police killed the suspects in a shootout inside our church building.

I arrived at our church, which was now a crime scene, to find the whole building surrounded and cordoned off.

"Two guys fled to your building, and it did not go well for them. They will not be walking out," a police officer told me.

After answering questions, I asked him when we could use our building.

"This is a crime scene, and you will not be able to go into the building for at least two weeks," he told me.

"But we have a big event planned for tomorrow, and it was not our fault they happened to run into our building," I said.

"I understand, and I'm sorry, but it is protocol. There's nothing we can do."

I called my lawyer, and we asked everyone to pray. Hours passed as we prayed and negotiated. At eight p.m., the police called and informed me we could have our building back.

"There is one condition," the officer said. "You will have to clean up if you want the building."

So my son and two other pastors donned protective clothes and rubber gloves and cleaned up the bloody mess left behind. I was proud they volunteered for this horrible job, but the reality of the violence around us was all too real. All of us—my family and I, my pastoral team, the young people present at the time, and our entire church—had to ensure our eyes were focused on Jesus, not the violence. Terror never leads to God's peace. It only distracts and paralyzes us, leading us to the wrong ways of thinking.

Never let fear or any other kind of wrong thinking get in the way of Jesus' invitation. As you focus on Him, replace negative thoughts about yourself with God-inspired, positive thoughts. Replace criticism and armchair quarterback behavior with genuine action. Replace an arrogant hero mentality with teamwork. Replace terror with courage, faith, and—most of all—love.

Once you learn the power of right thinking, you'll be dancing on water in no time.

CHAPTER 10
I'M DANCING NOW

The pastor informed me, "We're going to have to cut the support we send you each month."

I fought to maintain my composure as my mind raced. "Okay, I understand. How much do you need to cut?" I clung to a sliver of hope that it might be manageable.

His response came sharp and final: "All of it, of course."

Just like that, the financial lifeline I had depended on for twenty-two years was severed. I stood in stunned silence. That church had been my primary source of income for as long as I could remember. Now—without warning—it was gone.

The shock hit me hardest as I shared the news with my son and a few close staff members, each already carrying their own financial burdens. "I don't know what to do," I admitted, as the fear I'd tried to suppress rose to the surface. "Please pray for me."

As days turned into weeks, I wrestled with a storm of oppressive thoughts—visions of worst-case scenarios playing out in vivid detail. It felt like I could almost sense the same gusts of wind that made Peter falter when he stepped onto the sea. They were tugging at my spirit, threatening to pull me under.

But I recognized that wind for what it was: doubt. Whispering lies. Stirring fear and trying to shake my faith.

And then, in the middle of that internal storm, I remembered the truth: the Lord had never failed me. He had always been my Source, Rock, and Provider—through every high and low. No matter who He chose to work through or what means He used, my trust had never really been in man. It had always been in Him.

With that realization, a wave of peace washed over me. I let go of the fear, casting it aside, and rested in the assurance that His everlasting arms were still holding me.

Unexpected Phone Calls

The phone call that cut off my family's primary source of income came in December 2014 and the support ended at the first of the year. One month prior, I had received another unexpected call. When my U.S. phone rang that day, it surprised me—it was a rare occurrence that usually meant a solicitor was on the other end. *Another spam call*, I thought, ready to dismiss it. But something urged me to answer.

"Hello?"

A warm voice with a Hispanic accent came through the line. "My name is Jose. I'm calling from

Phoenix, and I can't seem to get your area out of my mind," he said. "Would it be alright if I came for a visit?"

"Absolutely!" I responded.

I seized the chance to invite him to our upcoming conference. He accepted the invitation, and a month later, he attended every session of our conference. Afterward, we sat in my office, discussing our great time and what God was doing in Tepic.

Jose's eyes filled with tears as he told me how he felt. "I don't know why," he admitted, "but I can't shake the feeling that the Lord wants me to move here to Tepic. Could I bring my family down and help out with the ministry? And there's one more thing—my business in Phoenix is doing well, and I feel led to send you ten percent of its income."

Shock and gratitude washed over me. "Of course," I said.

I could barely believe what I was hearing. As I waved goodbye, doubt immediately crept in. Was this going to happen? Uprooting his whole family felt like a distant possibility. But then, just two months later, his entire family arrived and settled into a house we had found for them to rent in Tepic.

The timing was so perfect that it had to be God, just like the story of the widow who sustained the prophet Elijah. Right when the income from the U.S. church dried up, this man's ten percent arrived—matching precisely what I had lost. The Lord had sent him right on time to provide what we needed. Despite everything, my income for that year remained unchanged. It was a testament to the Lord's provision, orchestrated in a way only He could.

Jose's support continued until the end of the year, and as it ended, I braced myself for what might come next. Then, another unexpected blessing arrived in December—a new source of funds designated to cover three full years of income! I was in awe, marveling at God's hand providing for us at every step.

> *I have been young, and now am old;*
> *Yet I have not seen the righteous forsaken,*
> *Nor his descendants begging bread.*
> *(Psalm 37:25)*

Now, I am dancing on the water! My income, my strength, and my wisdom come from the Lord. Together, we have weathered the fiercest storms—the 1994 devaluation of the Mexican peso, the global financial crisis of 2008, and the brutal drug cartel war that shook us from 2009 to 2012. We faced hurricanes, floods, and dangers lurking at every turn. But through it all, the Lord sustained us, holding us securely in His mighty arms.

To doubt Jesus now would be an insult—a betrayal of everything we have been through. Every new trial that comes will find me unshaken, my eyes locked on Him, joyfully dancing on the waves, confident that He will carry me through.

Nana's House

I could share stories of God's provision for days. One that is very special to my heart is how God provided land and a building for Nana's House, our orphanage.

The story began when my son offered to make two music videos for a well-known Christian musician if she would visit Tepic and perform a concert. At the time, we had no idea she was the governor's favorite musician; he used her song in his campaign. He even committed to come with his whole entourage. Her concert was a great success, and the church overflowed. After the event, the governor asked us to accompany him to dinner at his mansion.

The next night, we sat in the mansion waiting for him to arrive; politicians always arrive late. Dinner was tiring for me, as I had no desire to hear about all his successes. I was getting very frustrated. *Why am I even here?* I thought.

Then, the conversation shifted. As he talked about all his achievements, he mentioned a town where we work, and I seized the moment.

"We're doing a lot in Francisco I. Madero," I said, referring to the pueblo known as Puga. "We have a church there where we help children and Indigenous families. We run outreaches in several poor areas around the city." Then, I realized I was finally starting to enjoy the conversation.

"That's wonderful to hear. What do you need?" he asked.

That was the opportunity I had been waiting for. "We run our orphanage out of two rented houses," I explained. "We need land to build safe, permanent homes for the children."

Without hesitation, he replied, "If you need land, I will give you land."

The rest of the meeting was a blur. I could hardly contain my excitement—we had secured land for the children.

True to his word, the governor delivered, and soon we had land to build the orphanage. A talented local architect stepped forward and designed the plans for two new homes for free. Then, a church in Chicago, which often came to help us build our mission churches, offered to help us construct Nana's House. Their team was skilled and built the block wall around the property in one week. We started with ten thousand dollars, and their team gave even more on their trip to Mexico.

Then, it was time to begin construction. "We don't have a permit to build," I told my architect.

He replied, "Go ahead and build while we go through the permit process."

When our ten thousand was spent, thirty thousand came in from a wealthy friend in Mexico. Around that time, the architect told me, "You can only get the permit if you install the sewer lines."

This was the government's job, but they would not help. I soon learned that the nearest place to hook up to the sewer was three thousand feet away, and we had to install five manhole covers. Fortunately, our friends knew an engineer capable of doing the work. It was an eighty-thousand-dollar job, but they did it at cost, which came to thirty thousand dollars.

I never felt stressed about the project. We ran out of money at one point, so we waited until more came in. As we took one step at a time and walked on the water, we eventually raised over $250,000, and in December 2020, we moved into the beautiful new girls' home.

COVID-19

One of the fiercest storms we faced was the COVID-19 pandemic. In March 2020, I found myself preaching at a church in Oregon, and the air was charged with talk of a mysterious new virus from China. The unease was palpable, yet I didn't take it too seriously. In Mexico, handshakes and close contact are second nature—they are part of who we are—so when an elderly man at that Oregon church refused to shake my hand, I was taken aback. *Isn't this a bit of an overreaction?* I thought, puzzled by the anxiety that seemed to cling to the room.

When I finally returned home, the full impact of the situation hit me like a wave. What began as "two weeks to flatten the curve" was eight long months without a single in-person church service. The Mexican government enforced strict regulations, leaving no room for deviation. The consequences were severe—permanent closure and potential imprisonment for us as pastors if we failed to comply. So, with heavy hearts but faith built over years of experience, we shifted to online services, trusting Jesus to guide us through the storm.

But then came the greater challenge. In Mexico, the church depends on the tithes of its members, and most of our budget is dedicated to supporting our national pastors. With the congregation only gathering virtually, we faced a scary question: How on earth could we keep paying our staff when the church doors remained shut?

We gathered our leadership team, our hearts weighed down as we faced the frightening reality. Someone not at all encouragingly shared that "one large church in Mexico let go of their entire staff except for the Senior Pastor." That season felt like another step into the unknown, walking on water with nothing but faith holding us up. Yet, we did what we always do: we pressed forward, one step at a time, trusting God to make a way.

We reassured the staff, "We will continue paying everyone the same amount until we absolutely can't." Then we added, "Please give back whatever you can."

Amazingly, we never missed a single payday. Every Sunday, our staff faithfully showed up to run the online services, and devoted church members dropped off their offerings in person. When we finally reopened, we could only operate at thirty percent capacity. This limitation meant we had to restrict the number of attendees, but it didn't stop us. We held five services every Sunday to meet the demand.

> We pressed on, dancing through the storm, and by God's grace, He kept us afloat.

Looking back, I believe the pandemic was a direct attack on the church. At one point, authorities allowed bars to remain open while ordering churches to close their doors. But I clung to the promise that the gates of hell would not prevail against the church. So, we pressed on, dancing through the storm, and by God's grace, He kept us afloat through the unprecedented, two-year global crisis.

Although the devil meant it for evil, God even used COVID for our good. The crisis also allowed us to practice what we preach. We often talk about using what we have and not worrying about tomorrow or things beyond our control. I still joke about our five-year plans. COVID threw a wrench into all our plans, leaving us clinging to Jesus so we would not sink.

I Swallowed It

Why was there a nail in my mouth? I wondered. I was twelve years old, and I was sitting in the hospital, bewildered and anxious, beside my mother. As a child, I had an odd habit—something was always in my mouth. Later, I took up the harmonica, but before that, it was anything I could find.

While carrying boxes in the yard that day, something had gone wrong. I remember the moment vividly as if it played out in slow motion. The three-inch nail I'd been holding in my mouth suddenly slipped down my throat. Panic set in as I bent over, coughing and choking, but it was too late. The nail was gone.

"Mom, I swallowed a nail," I blurted out, fear gripping me.

We rushed to the hospital, my heart pounding in terror. After what felt like an eternity, the doctor finally called me in and asked what had happened.

"I swallowed a nail," I said, "and it's inside me right now."

The X-ray confirmed it—a ghostly outline of the nail lodged on the left side of my chest stood out starkly on the film.

"What do I do?" I asked.

The doctor looked at me with a calm expression. "This too shall pass." (I don't know if he used those exact words, but it was something close.) Then, with a slight smile, he added, "Literally. You'll need to wait until it comes out. Check every time you go to the bathroom so you know when it passes."

I nodded, though my mind was racing. I had a scuba-diving trip planned for ten days later, and the doctor's warning was clear: no extra physical activity until the nail passed to avoid the risk of it perforating my intestine. The countdown had begun, and I needed that nail out before my trip.

The next few days were the grossest experience of my young life. On the ninth day, I found it.

"Look, I found the nail!" I shouted as I waved the oxidized nail before my family. That long nail had passed through me, but I wouldn't have known unless I was willing to look for it.

I share this story not to gross you out but to make a point: sometimes, life sends you a lot of… uh…crap. But if you're willing to see past the smelly stuff, there is always good to be found.

Soon after I was saved, my church held a retreat at the seaside. "We are all going to meditate on a verse," the pastor told us, and he gave us Jeremiah 15:19.

> *Therefore thus says the L*ORD*:*
> *"If you return,*
> *Then I will bring you back;*
> *You shall stand before Me;*
> *If you take out the precious from the vile,*
> *You shall be as My mouth.*
> *Let them return to you,*
> *But you must not return to them."*

Notice the phrase "take out the precious from the vile." I memorized this verse and recall it often while dancing on the water. In every situation, I have learned to find something precious.

You probably remember Samson from the Book of Judges. Samson had a weakness for the ladies, and one day, on his way to visit his Philistine girlfriend, a lion suddenly leaped out, roaring and ready to attack. But at that moment, the Spirit of the Lord came powerfully upon him, and with supernatural strength, he tore the lion apart as if it were nothing. Later, Samson posed a riddle to the Philistines:

> *Out of the eater came something to eat,*
> *And out of the strong came something sweet.*
> *(Judges 14:14)*

In much the same way, we can take the attacks in our lives—the roaring lions—and transform them into something sweet. It's like learning to dance on water. Every hardship and trial holds a hidden sweetness, but it's up to us to uncover it. We sift through the rubble, separating the precious from the worthless, and discover the goodness that God has placed within even the fiercest battles.

Finding the ugly, smelly things in life—that's easy. But are we discovering the precious gems hidden within? That's the real challenge. Any fool can criticize, but who can spot the treasure in the mess?

Immature leaders often fall into the trap of thinking their only role is to point out and correct others' flaws. They may feel more spiritual because they can see the problems, but they fail to realize their true calling is uncovering something precious. Great leaders, on the other hand, are like treasure hunters. Instead of fixating on what's wrong, they search for the gifts, talents, and potential hidden within others. Their eyes are trained to see beyond the surface, recognize the beauty others might miss, and nurture it into something extraordinary.

The Grand Finale

All our years of walking on the water paid off. Although many fell by the wayside, we kept dancing on the water. The Apostle Paul wrote: "But we have this treasure in earthen vessels, that the excellence of the power may be of God and not of us. We are hard-pressed on every side, yet not crushed; we are perplexed, but not in despair; persecuted, but not forsaken; struck down, but not destroyed" (2 Corinthians 4:7-9).

When I look at our dance, I see the elements the Apostle Paul mentions—challenges, uncertainties, and seemingly impossible moments. But no matter how difficult the steps, Jesus always carries me through and makes the impossible possible.

How many people sink because they never learned to walk on the water? The Christian walk is based on faith. You start believing and finish believing.

At each stage and during every season, the Lord has upheld us, keeping us above the water and safe from the winds. Start by stepping out in faith if you want to live a supernatural life. Before you know it, you'll be dancing on the water too!

We've learned many dance moves on the water, and each step is a lesson in trust. In dance, the final moves have names—the grand finale, the finishing pose, and the closing move. But in life, no one knows precisely when their finale will come.

I want to finish the way I started: The just shall live by faith, walk by faith, fight by faith, and dance by faith. Like the Apostle Paul, I want a grand finale—one that echoes his words:

"I have fought the good fight, I have finished the race, I have kept the faith" (2 Timothy 4:7).

Will you hit the landing? Will you make the final pose?

This is a marathon dance, and it will come to a conclusion. I pray that you accept His invitation and jump in, knowing He upholds you. You trust Him to move every obstacle as you fix your eyes on Jesus.

I pray you never look back and never look down. That your thoughts remain on Him as you dance on the water—all the way to the end.

ABOUT THE AUTHOR

Dwight W. Hansen and his wife, Mary Jo, have been missionaries in Mexico since 1988 and are the founding pastors of La Fuente Ministries. Dwight directs Heart4Mexico, a U.S.-based nonprofit, while Mary Jo leads Nana's House orphanage.

Dwight ministers regularly in La Fuente's network of churches and is a sought-after speaker at churches and conferences worldwide. He is also the author of *Who Will Stay?: Building a House for the Presence of God in the World,* published in 2022 and available on Amazon and Audible.

Dwight and Mary Jo live in Tepic, Nayarit, where they enjoy life close to their two children and grandson.

ALSO BY D.W. HANSEN

God doesn't merely call us to go and preach the gospel, but also to stay, to love, and to build a House for His presence.

In *Who Will Stay?*, veteran missionary and church planter D.W. Hansen explains how the true power to change lives is found in community. Weaving together stories from the mission field and teaching from the Bible, he paints a picture of the House that Jesus is building: a safe, thriving, love-filled place where God's transformational work can flourish.

Available for purchase at amazon.com. Also sold in ebook and audiobook formats, as well as in Spanish.

ABOUT HEART4MEXICO

Since 1998, our nonprofit organization *Heart4Mexico* has assisted in providing life-giving transformation to Mexican communities through practical, Christ-centered ministries. These include church planting, an orphanage for children, an accredited School of Missions, and short-term missions teams. *Heart4Mexico* serves as a fountain of renewed hope and second chances to those we seek to serve, and we strive to maintain trustworthy standards and provide life-changing outcomes that will impact these communities for generations to come.

If you would like to support national pastors, missionaries, and projects, you can find more information or make financial contributions at h4mx.org.

Email: info@h4mx.org
Phone (US): 818-388-4835

www.ingramcontent.com/pod-product-compliance
Lightning Source LLC
LaVergne TN
LVHW020928090426
835512LV00020B/3256